BREAKTHROUGH!

A Complete Guide for Getting
Unstuck & Realizing Your Dreams

Victoria Loveland-Coen

Self-Mastery Press

Book design by Juliet Coen
Cover art by Hannah Harder
Interior design by Looseleaf Editorial & Production

ISBN (print): 978-1-7357645-0-4
ISBN (ebook): 978-1-7357645-1-1
Published by: Self-Mastery Press, P.O. Box 482, Carrboro, North Carolina 27510

This book is dedicated to all the New Thought pioneers who dared to question religious orthodoxy and boldly proclaim our oneness with the Infinite. We stand on your shoulders and continue your tradition of questioning accepted norms and attempting to discover Truth where it is ultimately found, within ourselves.

CONTENTS

INTRODUCTION

It was early fall. The Unity Minister's Regional Retreat had just concluded. It was a gorgeous time of year on a pristine lake in the mountains of Western North Carolina. The musical guest was awesome. The keynote was empowering. My workshop the day before was well attended and everyone reported that they received something truly valuable. Filled with an equal amount of joy and exhaustion, I walked back to my room after the evening program with a new member of our spiritual community. I liked this new member. She was sharp, stylish, successful, and had fallen in love with our community. I felt a friendship forming. When we reached the inn, she stopped me and said, "I hope you don't take this as criticism, but I have been wanting to ask you something."

"Ask away," I said, cautiously curious.

"Well, I've been thinking about our spiritual community, which offers a beautiful example of how to live lovingly and peacefully. It also teaches us how to use universal spiritual laws to achieve a joyous and successful life, and yet there are a lot of people who have been attending a long time, but they still seem to be struggling in one way or another, either with money, or relationships or career fulfillment. Why do you think that is, Victoria?"

I think I stumbled back a bit and took a long pause. It's not the first time I've been asked this. My husband has brought it up repeatedly. Secretly, I've questioned it myself. I've wondered why people who attend our service, even those who attend regularly, seem to

1

be stuck in the same place. Some do experience significant growth, and that's a beautiful thing to witness. But many still struggle with the same issues, year after year. I've always attributed it to how much effort the spiritual seeker actually brings to the table. There does seem to be a direct correlation between doing the work and experiencing transformation.

This is the answer I pulled out of my mental drawer and offered my friend. "It really comes down to how much the person is committed to doing the work . . . how committed they are to daily spiritual practice. Many people just come for the social aspect. It's great being around positive, heart-centered folks, and perhaps that's all they're looking for. Others are truly suffering and desperately want their lives to change. I see them attend Sunday service once or twice a month expecting some powerful juju to magically rub off on them. When it doesn't, they move on. 'Must be the spiritual community didn't really work for me,' they think, and choose another church, or try a different spiritual path, or new type of therapy. Yet, they remain stuck. I know because I've run into them—sometimes years later—and they're experiencing the same issues. They're really not committed to change."

That answer seemed good enough for the moment. We said good-night and I walked back to my room. I wanted to get a good night's sleep as I had a long drive ahead of me the next morning.

But I couldn't sleep. Her question kept rolling around in my mind. My answer seemed so incomplete, so feeble. "There's more to this, Victoria," I kept hearing in my head. "Yes, but what?" I know the "work in/transformation out" equation holds true for some. I have seen quite a few individuals, whose lives were in utter chaos, come into our spiritual center and begin to pour themselves into the classes, workshops, and group meditations. They do the work, commit to spiritual practices and, over time, their lives change—at least some aspects of their lives. There is commonly one thing that will not shift no matter how committed they are, and it is generally the one thing that, to them, is the most painful. This is when I hear the refrain, "Why isn't this working?"

Why, indeed? What does it take to break out of repeated patterns of lack, limitation, and loneliness? What is the "magic formula" for realizing our heart's true desires? There is none. Anyone who promises a magic formula is not being honest—at best. Believing that there is a "formula" for realizing our dreams and continuing to search for that elusive "magic pill" only keeps us trapped in our pain and can lead to self-loathing. We're tempted to think, even if unconsciously, "It must be me. I must not be doing it right." Or, "What's wrong with me; why can't I be more disciplined?"

What is the key that unlocks the prison in which many of us find ourselves, despite our efforts to visualize the good, affirm abundance, meditate, practice gratitude, create action plans, and implement those plans? These are the necessary tools, we're told, which will enable us to create the life of our dreams. And why, even when we've had a profound realization of our oneness with Source, does that not translate into an experience of unshakable peace and limitless funds in our bank account?

Why is healing elusive for so many? There is no simple answer, of course. Breaking free of long-standing issues that hold us back from living a joyous, love-filled, healthy, and successful life is a process that requires quantum growth in consciousness coupled with a commitment to spiritual practice. Ooh, there's that word, *commitment*. Why do so many have difficulty committing to practices they know will transform their life? Clearly, there is something essential missing.

My book reveals that missing piece by answering the question for all of you who are stuck, disillusioned, and crying out, "I'm doing the work, so why isn't it working?" If you're engaged in practical spirituality but are frustrated your expanded awareness is not translating into an experience of loving relationships, increased prosperity, success, and peace in your life, then read on. And, if you are new to a spiritual path, or to this way of thinking, then wonderful—you've got less to unlearn!

I know this because I missed it myself throughout the forty-plus years I've been on a spiritual path. Initiated into Transcendental Meditation at the age of sixteen, I have continued that practice all my life. When I was a teen, my mother and I attended a spiritual community in San Diego where I immersed myself in esoteric studies. I took classes in inner sensitivity, aura reading, and the power of the Divine Feminine. In the 1970s, I started doing yoga when it was still considered weird. It was in one of those classes, chanting "Om" with thirty other people, when I had my first mystical experience. I read all of Ernest Holmes's books, including *The Science of Mind* repeatedly throughout my twenties. I did EST (Erhard Seminars Training). In the late 1980s, I studied *A Course in Miracles* with Marianne Williamson when she lectured at the Preview House in Hollywood. I attended the professional Religious Science Practitioner Training at Agape under Rev. Michael Beckwith, becoming a licensed practitioner in 1997. After attending One Spirit Interfaith Seminary, I was ordained an interfaith minister in 2012. I've led a Unity congregation for eight years, and have taught meditation, as well as classes in prosperity, affirmative prayer, forgiveness, authentic living, and more. A few years later I was ordained as a Unity minister. I wrote a book and designed a program incorporating many of these teachings entitled, *Conscious Co-Creating*. Years of training and practice, and yet, there was an important piece I was missing.

I eventually grew by applying the spiritual wisdom I gained over the years, and saw that growth reflected in my experience. My commitment to daily spiritual practice keeps me centered in a peaceful, loving place...most of the time. In fact, in all but one area (which I discuss throughout the book), I had completely transformed my life. But it was a painfully slow process, one that included being stuck in the muck on quite a few occasions. And, as I previously mentioned, there was that one painful area that did not shift, despite my efforts to apply all the spiritual methods I knew. It did not shift *until I finally understood the missing piece and then developed practices that integrated that essential understanding.*

I slowly began to discover the whole premise of personal growth is flawed. Applying techniques of practical spirituality that we believe will change us, heal us, and bring us happiness are, at their core, misguided. It presupposes that we are "not okay" to begin with. It unintentionally sends a subliminal message that we are incomplete, don't have what we need, and must be fixed. It is this sense of "needing to be fixed" that keeps people trapped in a never-ending cycle of expectation and disappointment. That soul-crushing lie is just the beginning of the problem.

Breakthrough! reveals a comprehensive, step-by-step program for effectively releasing stuck energy that has choked off the growth of your authentic self, so you can embrace radical self-acceptance. You'll become aware of the pervasive influence of the collective unconscious and heal the patterns and shadows that have kept you stuck. As you begin to reintegrate your full self, you will discover and embrace the highest vision for your life, while learning to play in the energy of the answer. As a result, you will realize your full Divine Potential.

Know that my love and prayers are always with you on this journey. Let's get ready to set free your powerful and magnificent self and start living your dreams!

1

A HUNK OF ROCK
OR A MASTERPIECE
EMERGING?

*Self-acceptance, which is independent of the prase from the
outside world, accelerates our potential for growth because
it nurtures us from within.*

—Reverend Michael Bernard Beckwith

On a recent rainy Sunday afternoon, I found myself perusing the aisles of Barnes & Noble and came to the Personal Growth/Self-Help section. There before me was an entire aisle filled with books about all the different ways you can improve yourself. There were books on how to: overcome your bad habits, communicate better with others, have better relationships, be more successful in your career, achieve your goals, practice mindfulness, and be happier (lots of books on the latter topic). Then I noticed behind me an entire aisle of books just on the topic of how to lose weight and get in shape.

And it hit me, right there in the middle of Barnes & Noble—we are a nation of people who believe we're in need of being fixed!

Now, I'm all for being the best possible version of ourselves we can be. Absolutely. But unfortunately, the underlying message of all these books—and indeed the entire personal growth movement—is that we are not motivated enough, savvy enough, present enough, smart enough, skinny enough, rich enough, or loved enough. In short, *we are not enough*. And business is booming! Personal Growth is an $11 billion industry.

That got me thinking. Even practical spirituality can unintentionally send a subliminal message that there's something about us we need to change. If we think about practical spirituality in terms of using transcendent spiritual concepts for the purpose of healing our body, increasing prosperity, having more success in our work, or improving our life in general, we might be confirming our suspicion that we need fixing. Think about what brought you to a spiritual path. Many of us attend a spiritual center, or register for personal growth workshops or meditation retreats, or read books on practical spirituality for the purpose of healing something, or changing something about ourselves we don't like. Now, it's not the intention of New Thought to make us feel that we're not enough—not at all. The intention of this expansive way of thinking and experiencing Spirit is to awaken to an awareness of our innate Divinity and to align our thinking with Infinite possibilities. As a result, our lives naturally start to reflect that awakened consciousness. However, depending on where we are when we begin this journey of awakening, we can *unintentionally* receive the message that we are not okay as we are now. And that, right there, is the first thing that sabotages our efforts.

Again, it's not the *intention* of practical spirituality to make us feel "wrong." It's how, *and why*, we come to it. It's our *approach* that makes all the difference. If we begin by feeling deep down that there's something to be fixed, it won't matter how much we visualize, affirm, or pray; we'll never feel okay. Moreover, we'll be working against ourselves. It's one of the reasons people get stuck at some point on their spiritual path. It becomes a roller coaster ride of hopefulness and disappointment.

Have you ever had a profound realization of Truth, or learned about an exciting new method for realizing your dreams, and you invested yourself in doing all the prescribed practices? Perhaps you had some initial success and thought, "Yes, this is it!" But ultimately you discovered, much to your dismay, that it wasn't sustainable. Before long, you found yourself back in your old patterns of thinking and behaving.

Or, maybe the following describes your experience: You clear something up in one area of your life, and then another area pops up that needs work. So, you go to work on that, applying the spiritual principles you've learned, and you solve that problem. Soon, yet another problem pops up that needs work. After a while you realize you're playing a crazy game of New Thought "whack-a-mole." You become exhausted, and eventually disillusioned, trying to fix all the things you think are wrong in your life.

If you've spent any time on this roller coaster you might be tempted to think, "It must be me. I must not be doing it right. Maybe I'm just not disciplined enough." You beat yourself up for not being able to manifest like others seem to do. Conversely, some people assume it's the spiritual community they've been attending that's flawed, so they leave. They end up moving from one church to another, then another. Or, if they're adventurous, they might take the ride from New Thought to Buddhism, to crystal healing, to channeling, to Reiki, to psychotherapy, to mystical Kabbalah, to Wicca, to Shamanic trance traveling, to fill-in-the-blank—forever searching for that magic formula that will give them peace and transform their lives.

Now, any one of those paths could potentially bring you peace and joy. It's a question of motivation. *It's the place from which we begin our spiritual journey that determines our results.* If we continue to believe there's something to fix, that we're flawed, or our current experience is "wrong," we'll continue to create resistance. That resistance shapes an energy that keeps us repeating unproductive patterns. However, if our motivation is to know our Spiritual Self more fully, life will open to us so the magnificence that's already within us can emerge.

A MASTERPIECE UNFOLDING

I remember the day I began to understand this. It was as if I had woken up from a nightmare to find I was actually living a beautiful dream. It happened the moment after I spoke to my teacher at the Agape International Spiritual Center in Los Angeles, my spiritual community at the time. I tried to excuse my inability to commit to a particular spiritual practice by muttering something to the effect that I was "a work in progress." The teacher looked me right in the eyes and said, "No, Victoria, you're *not* a work in progress. You are a masterpiece unfolding." That one sentence struck me to my core and changed everything!

This is the awareness we want to open ourselves to—we are already complete and everything we need is within us. Now. We want to understand that the "masterpiece" within us is unfolding in the perfect way. I'm always inspired by what Michelangelo said when asked about his process for creating such beautiful masterpieces out of a hunk of rock. "I see the figure in the marble and I work to remove everything that doesn't belong in order to set him free." It's even more amazing that Michelangelo carved his statue of *David* out of a single piece of marble—one that had been discarded twice by other sculptors. If you've never seen the statue of *David* in person, it takes your breath away. You're not prepared for how large it is—its size doesn't come across in photos. The sculpture's size, grace, symmetry, and perfection will fill you with awe.

I have good news for you. (No, I'm not sending you to Florence to see *David* in person—it's something far better!) I'm giving you the straight up truth: you are, right now, a magnificent figure emerging from the most exquisite material, and not a hunk of rock that needs to be pounded endlessly to hopefully, one day, create something worthwhile! I want you to really hear that. You are, *right now,* an awe-inspiring masterpiece created by the ultimate master craftsman and are now engaged in a perfect process of emerging from Divine substance.

Also, the metaphor of "chipping away what doesn't belong" doesn't quite fit. It's more a process of lovingly releasing each piece that has been covering up your inner masterpiece and acknowledging the part it has played in your life, and then blessing it as you gently place those pieces aside. By doing so you honor your unique path, as well as everyone who has played a part in your drama. And that, as you'll discover in this book, is essential to your unfolding.

Embracing the totality of who you are, flaws and all, creates the conditions necessary to birthing your wholeness. Actually, it's the flaws in the marble that make it interesting and uniquely beautiful. In fact, those flaws, or *characteristics* in the marble, are created by intense heat and pressure. By honoring the "intense" experiences in your life, those "flaws" become your beautiful, distinctive *character,* sculpting the unique masterpiece that is you. When you learn to love the entirety of you, as well as your journey thus far, your Divine Self emerges fully, with all the uniquely beautiful textures that shape a remarkable life.

Now, I know you might be thinking, "How could I possibly love myself exactly as I am?" It turns out that's not such an easy task for those of us on a spiritual path. We tend to think, "If only I could meditate more regularly, or be more disciplined, or remember to breathe, or reconnect with my Spiritual Self more often, instead of coming from my fear and anger when 'that person' does 'that thing' that irritates me! *Then* I'd be okay. *Then* I'd be able to love myself more." But you see, the reason we don't remember, and we're not disciplined, is *not* because we're flawed. *It's because we don't love and accept ourselves completely.* You can't build motivation and discipline on top of self-contempt. You can't beat yourself into it!

I often think about those monks-in-training, who sit on a hard temple mat for hours in meditation with their gurus watching over them. When a monk begins to fall asleep, or starts to slump ever so slightly, the teacher comes by and whacks them on the back with a switch. Maybe that works temporarily to help train the mind to be more disciplined. But, ultimately, how effective is physical punishment in creating a peaceful mind and a loving heart? If you grew up Catholic or attended a parochial school, you might remember nuns rapping your knuckles with a ruler. Has that ever made anyone a better person? Beating ourselves up for being human is never a productive activity. These self-inflicted wounds can damage our sense of self and block our good. And yet, we do it all the time, albeit unconsciously. The voices in our head tell us we're not doing it right, we're not disciplined enough, smart enough, talented enough, skinny enough, relaxed enough, motivated enough, spiritual enough. In brief, we're *not enough*. These voices, as much in the background as they may be, eat away at the masterpiece that's yearning to emerge.

Many of these voices are simply echoes of well-meaning, but misguided, parents and teachers who unconsciously carry on the tradition of *their* parents and teachers. Well-meaning personal growth programs also unintentionally amplify this self-doubt. The seemingly endless number of self-improvement programs, workshops, webinars, telesummits, spiritual books, and personal growth gurus send a subliminal message, *we've been doing it wrong and we won't see success until we do it the way they prescribe.* Then, when our old patterns rise to the surface—as they will—we think we'll never succeed. It's mental self-flagellation. Ouch! No wonder we don't feel good about ourselves. No wonder it isn't working.

But we can choose to silence these judgmental voices now, both the external and internal ones. We can choose to see them for what they are—mistaken, unenlightened, counterproductive, and inaccurate.

AN UNEASY PATH

It took me a long time to learn to ignore the critics telling me I was doing it wrong, wasn't good enough, and was much too inexperienced. This "wisdom" seemed to be coming from people smarter and more experienced than me, so I listened. I began to internalize these critical voices until they became my own. Then I expanded their repertoire.

I moved to Los Angeles when I was 21 to pursue an acting career. With the exception of a few acting and stage production classes in college, I was a genuine newbie. Regardless, it was a career for which I initially believed I was destined. Before too long I found an awesome acting class on the backlot of Warner Bros. Studios. I was accepted into the class and dived right in. I loved it. I felt totally alive the entire time there, whether onstage doing scene work, or watching others bring the written word to life.

Three months into the class, a group of visiting producers and casting directors attended to watch us work. That night, I performed the best I ever had in the class. I've now forgotten the material, but I do remember the connection I had with my partner. It was magical. The next day, I received a call from a casting director who wanted me to come in and read for a movie they planned to film in South Korea starring Chris Mitchum, Robert Mitchum's son. Robert Mitchum starred in film classics such as *Cape Fear* (1962) and *Night of the Hunter* (1955).

When I arrived, I was told I was reading for the co-starring role. Imagine that: little, inexperienced me, given a chance like this! I was asked back several times to read for the producers and do a screen test. A few weeks later, I got the call saying I would play Nina, "the co-starring role opposite Chris Mitchum." How's that for beginner's luck! This was my big break. I was going to be a star! I remember what Marianne Williamson once said about beginner's luck: "You haven't learned the rules yet." In other words, you haven't learned all the "reasons" why you shouldn't have what you just got.

It wasn't until I arrived on the set in South Korea that I became aware of the status of this project. It was in chaos. No one knew what was happening and there wasn't enough money to make the film the way they envisioned. Everyone blamed everyone else. Me, being a newbie, got blamed a lot. "You're too subtle. We need to see you acting more...make it bigger!" This was the exact opposite of what I'd learned in class. I thought I was supposed to inhabit the character, really feel the emotions and let the camera pick it up. My inner critic kicked into full gear: *I must be doing it wrong. I'm wrong. I'm to blame.* That's when my budding anxiety truly blossomed.

The film was finally completed but never released in the United States—so much for my big break. The experience was over but my inner critic continued to tell me I wasn't good enough. Others amplified my fear by reminding me that getting a co-starring role right out of the gate is not how it happens. "You're supposed to pay your dues: start out with 'walk-ons,' then build to 'under-fives.' Climb your way up the ladder one rung at a time. And, by the way, since you didn't graduate from a prestigious drama school, your chances are slim. You know, Meryl Streep went to Yale." Oh, okay. I get it.

I got it all right. "Paying my dues" became my mantra for the next 10 years as I struggled to get cast in small roles, then beat myself up when I didn't even nail those. What's worse, I felt that if I wasn't a full-time working actor, making gobs of money, I was worthless. Low self-esteem, coupled with the hard-partying life-style of the L.A. film industry in the early '80s, was a recipe for disaster, and I fell right into it. To this day, I firmly believe it was my regular meditation practice that saved me from going right over the edge.

Another saving grace was a beloved book by Ernest Holmes, *The Science of Mind.* This book taught me how to do an Affirmative Prayer or "Spiritual Mind Treatment." I began to do this daily. The problem was, I was doing my prayer work from a place of seeing my desired good as "out there," while little worthless me "over here" was trying to pull the good into my experience. I wanted to manifest a brilliant career with big paychecks to feel better about myself, and so that others would accept me. But I couldn't accept myself. As a result, this spiritual practice only made me feel more separate from what I wanted...no, *needed*.

It took me years to realize these inner critical voices, coupled with a need for approval, were sabotaging my efforts and killing my dreams. Years later I finally realized what I was doing, then I worked to embody some audacious self-acceptance and an understanding that my life was perfect the way it was. Once that happened, everything shifted. My life began to reflect that inner transformation.

If you've been feeling stuck, if there's an area of your life that just doesn't seem to be shifting no matter how diligently you apply spiritual principles, if you've been unable to reach the next level of your spiritual growth, then here's the first key: You must begin to love yourself exactly as you are, knowing that all you need is already within you. Only when you embrace your journey and trust your guidance, will your inner masterpiece emerge perfectly and joyously. You can do it. This book can serve as your guide.

First, I want you to ask yourself: "Do I love myself completely, exactly as I am right now, where I am right now?" Be honest. You might think, "Well, I love myself when I'm meditating." Or, "I love myself when others are loving me." It's easy to love ourselves when we are immersed in a vibration of peace or surrounded by other people who love us. We all need that. It's important to dive into our inner peace and to surround ourselves with open-hearted, positive people. We want to drink this positive juice in and allow our batteries to recharge. But then we have to go back to our lives, our jobs, our relationships, our financial situations, and to all the people who don't necessarily love us. So, the question is, "Do you love yourself *then*?"

While I was contemplating this question one morning, an image came to me in meditation. As I share it, I invite you to join me on a journey of imagination.

Imagine you were just dropped into the middle of a tall maze in complete darkness. What's more, you think you need to find your way out of this maze without bumping into walls or taking too many missteps. It can't be done, right? Naturally you'll hit walls, stumble, and fall. You'll make wrong turns and venture into troublesome areas that lead you in the wrong direction. You might run into other people who will cause you to stumble, or purposely lead you down the wrong path. Eventually you pick yourself up, dust yourself off, and correct your direction. That's the only way any of us finds our way out of the maze! We don't beat ourselves up for it. We don't think less of ourselves because we couldn't get it right the first time. We understand what we're up against.

In a similar way, we are, at our essence, Divine Beings who have incarnated into a world asleep and dreaming a "dream of separation." In this pervasive dream, we experience being separate from our Source, separate from each other, and separate from our good. It's as if we've been dropped into a tall maze at night without a map. This is a foreign land for our soul. It's natural to hit walls, make wrong turns, doubt ourselves, and venture down troublesome trails.

But, there is a map! And it's our own internal GPS. We begin to hear that inner guidance system when we stop looking outside ourselves, or focusing on what's wrong, or what's missing. It becomes activated when we reconnect with the Self, shining brilliantly from the depths of our being. We cultivate that connection by loving each part of our journey and remembering that we have always done the best we could with the consciousness we have at the time. When we realize our life, thus far, has been the perfect *adventure* that has shaped the character of our masterpiece and given us a unique voice, our whole experience changes. Light illumines our path. We can clearly see the exit out of the maze. That light draws us toward our freedom, our joy, and the realization of our full potential.

Perhaps you are beginning to realize you've listened to voices telling you that you are wrong or that you are not enough. Maybe you're realizing that the search to fix yourself, or your life, has been part of the problem. Perhaps you're beginning to realize how loving and accepting yourself completely, and the entire marvelous and messy journey you're on, might allow the masterpiece you truly are to fully emerge. So, now you're wondering, "How do I even begin a process like that? I've spent my entire life judging myself. I've made too many mistakes. My parents' critical voices are deeply embedded in my psyche. In fact, I have a whole committee of voices convincing me I'm not quite enough. But maybe if I keep working on myself—." You wonder how you can quiet these voices. How do you do that?

Let's pull some wisdom from psychologist Gay Hendricks, who writes about his journey of self-acceptance in his classic book, *Learning to Love Yourself*:

> I realize that there is nothing that really needs to be done
> in learning to love ourselves other than to be willing to
> love ourselves. We have spent so many years being un-
> willing to love ourselves that to simply turn it around
> and be willing to love sets in motion a tide of energy that
> will carry us along.[1]

It begins with a willingness . . . just a *willingness* to love yourself and your journey. A good place to start is by exploring those places where you feel like you're stuck. What do you think isn't working? Where do you find that, despite your efforts, things are not moving forward? Give some space to these feelings. See if you can uncover what you haven't been able to love. Have you become impatient about your progress, or with yourself? Do you sense that you will never be enough until you achieve something, find the right partner, or make a certain amount of money? How do you feel about yourself without those things? Would you be willing to love yourself if you never achieved the things you think are missing from your life? Alternately, have you tried pretending that not having what you truly desire doesn't really bother you ("I didn't really want to get married anyway") but, deep down, it really hurts? Do you think you could be willing to love the place within you that feels unworthy of having a full, love-filled, and successful life? Remember, all it takes is *willingness*. You can even love your *resistance* to loving it. By loving it, you give it space and allow it to be. Those painful places then start to open and might even reveal something important. George Washington Carver once said, "Anything will give up its secrets if you love it enough...when I silently commune with people, they give up their secrets too, if you love them enough." So, be willing to love the places where you feel stuck or unworthy. Be willing to love those places where you tried to apply spiritual principles but didn't see results. Your willingness to love yourself and the places you feel stuck will allow its secrets to be revealed to you. Following is an exercise that will help you with this process.

LESSON ONE, EXERCISE ONE: LISTENING TO THE PAIN

To access the guided process, go online to Breakthrough2.com/exercises and click on Lesson 1, Exercise 1. Alternatively, you can read the following instructions first and then close your eyes and begin the exercise. Or, have someone read it to you while you do it.

Have on hand a piece of paper or your journal, and a pen or pencil. Find a quiet space and get comfortable. Begin by taking some slow deep breaths. Close your eyes, and allow your breath to move your awareness from your thinking mind down into your heart center. This is where your Inner Wisdom dwells. Allow the love that resides in your heart center to begin to emanate out, filling your entire body. With each breath, feel that love radiating through your very being as it intensifies. Allow yourself to feel that radiant love for a few breaths.

Now, bring to mind that place where you feel stuck, where things don't seem to respond to your efforts, or where you feel inadequate, or unworthy of having the realization of your dreams. When you have that place in mind, envision that image at the center of your heart. You might want to see it as a hunk of marble that has been covering up your masterpiece-self. Imagine the radiant light and love of your inner Divine Self surrounding that piece of marble, which represents your issue, with infinite love. Envision this Divine Self permeating that issue—be it physical, emotional, relationship, career, financial, or personal—with unconditional love. That loving energy is surrounding and penetrating the very core of this painful experience. Imagine now that this area is beginning to open with the love that is infusing it. Feel it begin to soften. Sense the pain dissolving and the resistance loosening. Become aware that any sense of unworthiness is now melting in the warm glow of Infinite Love. See yourself being willing to accept *you* exactly as you are, with this issue. Feel it all softening with Divine Love. You might even begin to notice all the unique and beautiful marbled textures and characteristics you never noticed before. Can you see it? Take a few moments and observe the beauty in yourself.

Now ask your Inner Wisdom the following questions:

- What have I accepted as true about me?
- What message does this issue have for me?
- What gifts has this painful place been holding for me?
- How can I grow from this experience?

Be open, observe, and listen. Give it time. Once you've received something, open your eyes, take your journal out and write it down. The process of writing it down will further clarify the message.

You can repeat this exercise, offering up each area in which you feel stuck or unworthy.

LESSON ONE, EXERCISE TWO: FEEL THE LOVE

The guided version of this exercise is also on the website Breakthrough2
.com/exercises: Lesson 1: Exercise 2.

This exercise may bring up some pretty deep emotions. That's okay. Try to
stay open and let them flow. Know that Infinite Love supports you. Experience the peace in release.

Begin as you did in the first exercise in a meditative or relaxed state. Close
your eyes and start taking some slow deep breaths. Once again, allow your
breath to move your awareness from your thinking mind down into
your heart center. When you feel relaxed and present, imagine a Divine Presence standing directly behind you—this could be any heavenly being with
whom you resonate. Perhaps it's Jesus or Buddha or Green Tara. If there is
a guru you relate to, imagine your guru standing behind you. This Divine
Presence could also take the form of a Goddess, an angel, or an Earth Deva.
Or, if you'd prefer, it could just be loving, positive light-energy.

Now, envision yourself either immersed in this positive light-energy, or
imagine the Divine Presence embracing you and pouring Its love into your
heart. Feel that love permeating your entire being. Imagine that love infusing the darkest corners of your being. Sincerely open your mind and heart
to allow this healing love to penetrate through all your layers. If thoughts
come to mind that say, "Oh, I won't let you see that because it's too ugly.
It's too unlovable. I've done things I'm ashamed of," then imagine that
Divine Presence loving you even more—every part of you, and holding
you as you release this painful memory. Remember that Divine Presence
knows about the "tall maze" into which you've been dropped. Trying to
hide all the crazy places, and all the "flaws," has taken so much of your energy. Now you can let it go and free up that energy for your glorious life.
Take some time to breathe through this until you can feel that infinite love
penetrating every corner of your mind...every part of your psyche...every
inch of your body...every memory from your past. Accept the cleansing
light from that Divine Presence completely dissolving all judgment and
self-criticism. All that remains is pure love—for yourself and the sweet
honoring of your unique path.

When this feels complete, take a deep breath, open your eyes and come back into the here and now.

You have just taken the first step on the journey of loving and accepting the fullness of who you are. Perhaps you are starting to see how every path you've taken has contributed to creating your beautiful, unique expression. Each experience has added exceptional texture and character to your masterpiece. The entire adventure has helped to craft the inimitable gifts that you are here to share with the world. By sharing your unique gifts, you will be honoring your path and doing your part in making a positive difference in the world.

You're now ready to continue your journey out of the maze. You will learn to embrace the "Spectrum of Oneness" that you are, release toxic energy that is blocking your good, effectively recover from the influence of the collective unconscious, reintegrate your full Self, and learn to play in the energy of pure love and joy—all of which will allow the full emergence of the magnificent life that is waiting for you.

2

EVOLVING OUR FOUNDATION

Ancient Seeds

*Faith looks to the invisible and instead of seeing a void,
it fastens its gaze upon a solid reality.*

—Ernest Holmes

Change your thinking, change your life. Affirm the best! Develop an attitude of gratitude. Utilize the power of positive thinking. Expect a miracle! I'll see it when I believe it. We are all one. We are spiritual beings living in a material world.

These pithy phrases are so commonplace today they've become bumper stickers. Clichés. We tend to think they're simply a product of our current culture, encouraged by such popular figures as Deepak Chopra, Wayne Dyer, or Oprah. But, actually, the core truths behind these ideas have been with us for a long time. They are strands of a larger tapestry woven with golden threads from an ancient era, fully emerging as the New Thought movement in the mid-nineteenth century.

This chapter puts into historical context the evolution of some of the most mind and soul-expanding ideas that, when embraced, have the power to transform lives. You will deepen your understanding of proven methods, and the philosophy behind those methods, to help you break free from ineffective patterns, and allow your full magnificent self to shine. It's affirming to realize that, throughout the ages, thousands of others have done the same by applying these core ideas and healing methods. Indeed, we stand on the shoulders of many individuals, no different than ourselves, who stood boldly in their Spiritual Identity and called forth the realization of their highest Divine Potential.

As far as we know, this rich tapestry of transformational ideas began in ancient India. Vedic texts expressed the core concept of "non-duality" perhaps for the first time. Non-duality is the view that there is no "other"—the dichotomy between you and I, or *it*, is transcended.

No one knows exactly when the Vedas were written, or by whom, but estimates place them anywhere from 1500–1000 BCE. In the Upanishads (written circa 800–200 BCE), sacred essays re-interpreting Vedic thought, we find, "To the seer, all things verily become the Self; what delusion, what sorrow, can there be for him who beholds that oneness?"

This theme of non-duality, or "oneness," is the core idea from which the New Thought movement grew. In fact, part of what made this movement "new thought" was that its proponents re-jected the idea of duality. They disavowed the common wisdom of the day that espoused a belief in a deity outside of and separate from ourselves. Instead, they embraced a more expansive idea of oneness with the Universal Self.

The profound wisdom of the Ancient Vedas influenced many systems of thought throughout the world. Early translations of Vedic texts reached America's shores in the late 1700s, falling into the hands of inquisitive individuals to include Ralph Waldo Emerson's father, William Emerson. Perhaps he planted those ancient seeds of "oneness consciousness" in his son's mind. The younger Emerson grew to embody the Vedas' wisdom and would later share Vedic-inspired ideas that, "The material universe is an emanation of divine power and that the purpose of human life is for the soul to realize its inherent unity with its source." Secondly, he acknowledged the concept of *maya*, "the multiplicity of forms as a kind of illusion that obscures the knowledge of oneness." (More on Emerson later.)

Vedic wisdom also influenced Ancient Greece. Plato gave us the understanding of metaphysics and wrote about the illusory nature of the visible world. He believed that reality could be found only in the invisible, while all visible forms of life are only copies, or shadows, of the real world. It is in the invisible where the ideal of perfection is found. And that dimension cannot be accessed by our senses. In fact, according to Plato, our senses trap us into a world of illusion. Plato's "Theory of Forms," which began to spread through-out the entire Hellenistic world, would centuries later weave its threads into the tapestry that became the New Thought movement.

Around that same time (500 BCE) emerged Siddhartha Gautama, who would be called the Buddha. In the Dhammapada, a collection of Buddha's sayings distilled from the larger Pali Canon, we find profound wisdom whose impact can be felt today in progressive spirituality. The very first saying in the Dhammapada is:

> All experience is preceded by mind,
> led by mind,
> made by mind.
> Speak or act with a corrupted mind,
> and suffering follows
> as the wagon wheel follows the hoof of the ox.
>
> All experience is preceded by mind,
> led by mind,
> made by mind.
> Speak or act with a peaceful mind
> and happiness follows
> like a never-departing shadow.

Herein lies a major tenet of New Thought—all experience originates in the mind. As we begin to think thoughts of oneness and perceive all of life with a loving heart, we experience happiness.

The Buddha also gave us the practice of meditation, which countless individuals have since used as a tool for accessing that "invisible realm," or what we might now refer to as the Absolute Realm of the Infinite. Meditation is positively central to the New Thought movement.

Woven deeply into this rich tapestry of New Thought are the teachings of Jesus. Many believe that Jesus was the prime example of one who lived completely from a consciousness of oneness, and therefore was the ultimate teacher and "wayshower." Not all proponents of New Thought believe in or relate to Jesus; nor is it necessary to believe to be a "New Thought person" or to benefit from these expansive ideas. However, intertwined throughout this philosophy are some of Jesus's original, radical, and deeply transformational ideas such as: "The Kingdom of God is within you;" "With God all things are possible;" and "Pray believing and ye shall receive." These ideas were embraced by New Thought pioneers who looked at the Bible a bit differently than traditional

Christians—they saw biblical stories as metaphorical and viewed the complete work through a metaphysical lens. While some in New Thought saw Jesus as a representational construct, others saw Him as a historical figure—a man who reached the highest heights and came to show us how to heal. Still others saw Him as a fully realized Divine Being, present and available to us now. From either perspective, He was not seen as the sole Christ, but as someone who came to show us how to think correctly, love unreservedly, and awaken to the Christ within ourselves. The understanding is that when we embody Jesus's teachings, we will experience the Heaven that "is at hand." The Apostle Paul (Romans 12:2) give us a clue for doing this: "Be ye not conformed to this world, but be ye transformed by the renewing of your minds."

New Thought pioneers understood this to mean that we renew our minds by looking beyond the *appearances* of the physical world to remember who we truly are. This creates a shift in consciousness, which transforms *us*, and therefore our experience. When we no longer accept limitations as defined by the world, but instead are open to an expanded view of ourselves, we become liberated. And as Thoreau said, "We may live with the license of a higher order of beings."

We'll fast-forward through the Middle Ages, where these ideas seem to have gone underground for the most part, with the notable exception of an impressive list of mystics, whose expansive awareness shone like bright lights dotting a rather spiritually bleak period. They included Pseudo-Dionysius the Areopagite, John Scotus Erigena and Meister Eckhart, among others. Non-conforming mystics sprung from all faiths, including Judaism, Christianity, Hinduism, Buddhism, and Sufism. Probably best known today is the thirteenth-century Persian poet, Rumi. In Rumi, there is transcendent wisdom that cuts across all boundaries of culture and religion, and has resonated with countless individuals throughout the ages. In just a few select words, he sums up our relation to the whole. "You are not a drop in the ocean. You are the entire ocean in a drop." Take a moment and contemplate the wisdom of those words. You are not an insignificant speck of dust in a vast universe. You are whole universe expressing as an individual.

In Europe, around the eighteenth century, emerged regular questioning of entrenched institutional religious beliefs and a growing desire to have a direct experience of the Divine. These ideas formed a new philosophy that would feed into the formation of New Thought. Major influences included Emanuel Swedenborg of Sweden, Rudolf Steiner of Austria, Germany's Georg Hegel, and Judge Thomas Troward of England. Their experiences and writings began to spread around the world. But nowhere was the growth of these ideas more prominent than in America, where new ideas could breathe and grow.

THE TRANSCENDENTALISTS

This brings us to the Transcendentalism movement, possibly the greatest spark that lit the flame of the New Thought movement. From the Transcendentalists came radically new ideas that began to change the intellectual landscape in America. Ralph Waldo Emerson, Henry David Thoreau, Margaret Fuller, and John Muir were all individualists who parted with the traditional religious doctrine and rationalism of the Enlightenment; they each turned to nature and their own mind and soul for truth and inspiration.

Transcendentalism claimed for *all* what traditional Christianity claimed only for the "saved." The Transcendentalists were also early feminists. As Charles Braden writes in his book, *Spirits in Rebellion*, "It was the logical result of the Transcendentalist belief that souls were of no particular sex. Men and women were alike human beings, with all their human capacities, longing and destiny and should enjoy equal rights." Perhaps it was this idea of women's equality that paved the way for the many women who were to become leaders in the movement. New Thought was the place women could have a voice *and* take the lead.

Emerson, in particular, came to the understanding that all human beings are an integral part of the Divine. In his famous essay, *The Over-Soul*, he writes: "There is no bar or wall in the soul, where man, the effect, ceases, and God, the cause, begins. The walls are taken away. We lie open on one side to the deeps of spiritual nature, to the attributes of God."

As mentioned earlier, Emerson was influenced by Eastern thought. He began reading translations of the Vedas while a teenager. His reading list was quite extensive, with topics ranging from Christian theology, philosophy, science, and natural history, to a wide variety of sacred spiritual texts from around the world. He was even influenced by the thinking and traditions of Native Americans and spoke out against their mistreatment. From these varied sources he began to center his beliefs around a core idea of non-duality. Emerson writes in *The Over-Soul*:

> We live in succession, in division, in parts, in particles. Meantime within man is the soul of the whole; the wise silence; the universal beauty, to which every part and particle is equally related; the eternal ONE. And this deep power in which we exist and whose beatitude is all accessible to us, is not only self-sufficing and perfect in every hour, but the act of seeing and the thing seen, the seer and the spectacle, the subject and the object, are one.[1]

It's surprising to read such enlightened, cutting edge thinking that seems as if it could have been written today, but Emerson wrote it in 1841. For most of the world, Emerson's ideas were revolutionary. And yet this passage echoes ancient Vedic ideas like the one previously quoted, "To the seer, all things verily become the Self; what delusion, what sorrow, can there be for him who beholds that oneness?"

This understanding is as old as time because it is embedded in our Soul. It strikes a chord deep within us that awakens a universal wisdom. And when we stay awake to that wisdom, we open ourselves to a more expansive experience of life.

As New Thought developed, the goal of these progressive spiritual pioneers was to take the profound ideas the Transcendentalists were expressing and make them practical. They created a way to apply these spiritual concepts to their day-to-day lives to heal illness, mend relationships, and live a more abundant life. If it was not practical, they thought, it was just theory—a lovely sounding idea, good to meditate on—but if I'm sick, or can't pay my bills, or my living situation is impossible, how are these lofty ideas serving me?

Soon a system for making those ideas practical began to emerge from a very unexpected place.

MIND-CURE

In the early to mid-1800s in New England, where the New Thought movement had its roots, *mesmerism* (also known as animal magnetism) was all the rage. In fact, the term mesmerism came from an eccentric German doctor, Franz Anton Mesmer, who experimented with methods of putting people into a trance-like state and giving them suggestions. His theory held that a mysterious fluid flowing through the body could be manipulated, *through his mesmeric suggestions*, to heal people of any number of maladies.

Mesmer was later accused of being a fraud, but the fascination with mesmerism continued. Eventually scientists began to study it. They experimented with putting subjects into a deep, relaxed state, while giving them suggestions that would cause physical conditions to occur, such as raising blisters, altering their blood flow, and disrupting their circulation and digestion. James Braid, a Scottish surgeon, was among those experimenting with this new system. He concluded that indeed this was a real phenomenon, but not because of a mysterious fluid. It was the power of suggestion at work. He is credited for naming this approach to healing *hypnotism*. Braid also discovered this suggestable state could be self-induced, thus self-hypnosis.

These experiments initiated the idea that healing could occur through non-medical, purely mental means. It was in this environment that the American, Phineas P. Quimby, now thought of as the founder of New Thought, appeared onto the scene. Quimby happened to attend a demonstration of hypnotism in New England that captured his imagination. He studied all he could about the topic, then opened his own practice as a "mesmeric healer." Quimby was feasibly the first to confidently state a concept that others only guessed was happening—that erroneous thinking, fear, unforgiveness, guilt (including religious guilt), and long-held beliefs rooted in duality, contributed in large part to the manifestation of disease. He writes in his collection, *The Quimby Manuscripts*, "Man is made up of truth and belief; and if he is deceived into a belief that he has, or is liable to have, a disease, the belief is catching and the effect follows it." Quimby understood that by fully accepting the true relationship of the Divine and man, we heal. He believed God to be "invisible wisdom, which fills all space, and whose attributes are all light, all wisdom, all goodness and all love . . ."

Quimby's philosophy and practice developed over time and his hypnosis healing eventually evolved into a technique he called "mind-cure." He took the idea that "all experience originates in the mind" (remember, from the Buddha) and helped his patients ease into a receptive frame of mind by directing their focus on thoughts of wholeness. He helped them embody the truth that well-being was their innate state. Once they were totally convinced of that, the experience of illness would resolve itself and health was revealed.

If this idea sounds familiar, it may be because it's coming back around—this time promoted by a few popular authors who have been backing up their claims with cutting-edge scientific evidence. Joe Dispenza incorporates brain scans to prove the efficacy of a complete focus on well-being. Bruce Lipton and Gregg Braden study the effects of belief on our genes. It's affirming to finally have scientific evidence for healing methods that were personally proven to the individuals who practiced them well over a century ago.

Quimby's practice flourished and hundreds of people claimed to be healed by him using this method. Perhaps the most well-known person who came to him for healing (and once healed, studied with him) was Mary Baker Eddy. She would later deny that she was treated by Quimby or learned this technique of mind-cure from him, and claim that these truths were revealed to her alone. She took those ideas, anchored them firmly in biblical accounts of healing through faith, and then went on to found Christian Science.

For a variety of reasons, Christian Science is not considered to be part of the New Thought movement, although they have similar roots. The most apparent difference is that Christian Science refuses medical intervention, while those who were part of the developing New Thought movement saw the assistance of medical doctors as another effective way innate wholeness is revealed. Even though they regarded the task of "renewing of the mind" primary to healing, medicine could work in harmony with that shift in consciousness.

The other clear difference is that Christian Science is a closed system. For example, their services today are exactly the same as those given by Mary Baker Eddy 150 years ago. No new ideas are allowed. In contrast, New Thought is "open at the top"—the movement welcomes new ideas and is constantly developing within an evolving collective consciousness.

Another important beneficiary of Quimby's healing and teaching was Warren Felt Evans, whose major contribution to the New Thought movement was in documenting the exciting work of Quimby, and others, who used spiritual mind techniques. Evans wrote articles and books with stories of the New Thought healers' successes. He was the first to articulate a specific philosophy incorporating these thought-provoking ideas. His work circulated widely, and the movement began to take off.

A big fan of Emanuel Swedenborg, Evans blended metaphysical biblical interpretation with mystical revelation, as this passage from his book, *The Primitive Mind Cure*, reveals:

> That all there is or can be in what men call heaven is already in us, like the miniature plantlet in the seed of the sacred lotus. It is there as a celestial germ. The kingdom of God is within. This narrows down our search for it to a small compass, and heaven is at hand or within our reach. And surely, where heaven is there must be health and happiness...which in their very essence are one, are always within us, and can never by any possibility be external to the mind. To believe this is to find them.[2]

This passage echoes Jesus's instruction to look, not here or there, but within: "The kingdom of Heaven is within you." (Luke 17:21) While this statement is quite clear, traditional Christians have, for centuries, conceived of Heaven as a place somewhere in the sky, where they'll go after they die *if* they haven't committed a mortal sin. Again, New Thought pioneers dug deep into the original meaning of spiritual masters like Jesus to find a higher truth. Evans helped to expand that understanding for his readers.

Evans synthesized "mind-cure," along with metaphysics and mysticism, into a working system, giving people the power to heal themselves of illness and live joyous and fulfilling lives.

NEW THOUGHT TAKES OFF

Perhaps the person most responsible for spreading New Thought ideas throughout the United States was Emma Curtis Hopkins, a former student of Mary Baker Eddy, who left Eddy's authoritarian rule in order to explore her own internal compass. Hopkins was a true mystic, healer, and teacher, who soon established her own school in Chicago. She successfully cured nearly everyone who came to her. But for her, healings were only a prelude. Her true goal was to see this new movement grow. Her mind was sharp and the depth of her spiritual understanding profound. She became known as the "teacher of teachers" because the way she communicated this wisdom to others quickened their understanding. She actively empowered her patients/students to form centers or organizations where they too could teach and spread this philosophy throughout the United States.

Among her students were Annie and Harriet Rix, who, together with Malinda Cramer, founded Divine Science and took it to the West Coast. Althea and Nona Brooks expanded their brand of Divine Science to Colorado. H. Emilie Cady, an early writer of Unity textbooks, was also a student of Hopkins, as were Charles and Myrtle Fillmore, who brought their version of New Thought to the Midwest. A couple decades later, Ernest Holmes studied with Hopkins, deepening his understanding, which established him as a leading spiritual teacher in Southern California.

As an early feminist, Hopkins appointed women to prominent positions in her institution, the Emma Hopkins College of Metaphysical Science. As early as 1889, her seminary graduated twenty-two students, twenty of whom were women. In her writings, she often used female pronouns to describe the Holy Spirit.

Like New Thought pioneers before her, Hopkins also viewed Jesus's teaching with a mystical and metaphysical eye and referenced his teachings throughout her writings. But unlike Mary Baker Eddy, Hopkins did not hesitate to incorporate wisdom from the Greek philosophers and the Vedanta, as reflected in this passage from her book, *Scientific Christian Mental Practice*:

> The Eastern mystic repeats the word "OM" by drawing in his breath and speaking the word twelves times. Then he holds his breath and repeats the word twenty-four times. Finally, he feels that he himself is "OM." To feel that OM is your substance, your life, your mind, is greater than to feel that the words you say are OM. The only words you can speak and be identified with, wisely, are, "I am my own understanding of God."[3]

"I am my own understanding of God" is a powerful statement that appears repeatedly in Hopkins's writings. While in truth we are "OM," or we are "God" expressing, we experience that reality only to the degree of our understanding. And that, in a nutshell, is New Thought. The pioneers of this movement knew that their work was to increase understanding of the true nature of being. Only by fully embracing our oneness with the One can we accept the joy, well-being, and abundance that is ours.

That same idea, expressed from a different perspective by the aforementioned H. Emilie Cady, had a major impact on the philosophy of New Thought, chiefly in her book, *Lessons in Truth*. The text was originally a series of "lessons" published by Charles and Myrtle Fillmore in their magazine, *Modern Thought*, in the late 1890s. In it Cady writes,

> You may say to yourself...over and over again, that you are well and wise and happy. On the mental plane, a certain "cure" is effected, and for a time you will feel well and wise and happy. This is simply a form of hypnotism, or mind-cure. But until, down in the depths of

your being, you are conscious of your oneness with the Father, until you know within yourself that the spring of all wisdom and health and joy is within your own being, ready at any moment to leap forth...you will not have spiritual understanding.[4]

Cady noticed, even then, that followers and even practitioners of this movement were sometimes using these "mental healing methods" in a superficial way and therefore not having the success they hoped for. Isn't it funny that, more than a century later, people still repeat affirmations like magical incantations, expecting their circumstances to change. As Cady understood, in order to free ourselves, we must make a complete shift in our understanding and know that, "down in the depths of our being," we are that One expressing.

Once we fully realize and embrace the reality of who we are, we can move to the second part of that practical, working formula. Cady points the way in this passage:

One of the unerring truths in the universe is that there is already provided a lavish abundance for every human want. In other words, the supply of every good always awaits the demand. Another truth is that the demand must be made before the supply can come forth to fill it. To recognize these two statements of Truth, and to affirm them, [is] the whole secret of understanding faith—faith based on principle.[5]

Over the course of the late nineteenth and early twentieth centuries, there were many others who contributed to the formation of New Thought through their writings, teachings, and healing demonstrations. Some organized into schools or spiritual centers. Several, such as The Metaphysical Club of Boston, Greenacre Conference, Madame Blavatsky's Theosophical Society (although not technically New Thought), Homes of Truth, and Divine Science centers, enjoyed robust attendance in their day. However, the two organizations that formed around this time—and continue to thrive even today—were Unity and, a little later, Religious Science (now known as Centers for Spiritual Living).

Unity (originally Unity School of Christianity) grew in Kansas City, Missouri, from the hearts of two loving individuals after each experienced a spectacular healing. Myrtle Fillmore was cured of life-threatening tuberculosis after hearing a lecture by E. B. Weeks, a student of Hopkins, which led to an epiphany. In that talk, Weeks stated, "I am a child of God, and therefore I do not inherit sickness." That struck a chord in Myrtle and she took it to heart. She began working with this affirmation. She didn't just repeat it, but worked diligently to embody the Truth behind those words in all levels of her being. Within two years, she was completely free of the disease. Her full healing inspired her husband Charles to open to these ideas, and he, too, experienced a healing of his leg that he had injured as a boy.

Charles Fillmore had an interesting childhood, having been raised in a small town in Minnesota. With a keenly curious mind, and not many friends to play with, Charles read an extraordinary number of books. Befriending a woman who owned a library filled with esoteric spiritual and religious texts, he educated himself in the tenets of each of the world's religions. Although raised Christian, there remained a definite Indian essence that eventually permeated much of his writings. That Eastern influence is particularly apparent in his theory of the 12 Powers—twelve "energy centers" in the body that, when activated, become access points to greater spiritual power. What is that but another way to understand the chakras?

Myrtle had a college education, but not the kind of access to world religious texts like Charles did. Still, she was a deeply spiritual woman. Living in the Midwest at the beginning of the twentieth century, the Fillmores instinctively knew that for a spiritual organization to survive and thrive, it would need to be based in Christianity. And, like most New Thought leaders of the day, the Fillmores viewed the Bible with a metaphorical or metaphysical eye. In fact, Charles wrote an entire Metaphysical Bible Dictionary, reinterpreting biblical stories, places, and characters in a unique, symbolic way that gives present-day readers touch-points for their own spiritual growth. He, too, saw Jesus as a "wayshower" who came to awaken the Christ in all. In his book, *Christian Healing*, Charles states clearly, "The ability of the individual mind to combine the ideas of Divine Mind in a consciousness of its own makes each of us the 'only begotten Son,' a particular and special creation."

Myrtle was profoundly devoted to helping others understand these teachings and have an experience of their own spiritual reality. She writes in one of her letters to an individual requesting prayer:

> In reality man's higher Self is spiritual. He is Life and Intelligence expressing. He thinks and his thought becomes objective as form. These forms are of many grades of density, or as the physical scientist would say, molecular vibration. The real man is not any of these forms; he is the force that causes the forms to exist, and when he knows this, every phase of phenomenal life comes under his dominion.[6]

Here we begin to see the concept of a vibrational world of varying density that responds to our conscious direction. We'll explore this idea more fully in the next several chapters.

Together, Charles and Myrtle Fillmore began to share these ideas through their magazine and letters, eventually forming Silent Unity, an organization dedicated to using the techniques of Affirmative Prayer to help others. Many visited the Fillmores at their home with requests for healing. Charles, in particular, worked with individuals day and night to help bring about a healing utilizing these methods; he was successful in many cases.

Charles had a creative mind and worked out many theological and philosophical questions, including: "If we are all expressions of the One, why don't we know that?" His answer:

> This question naturally presents itself: If we are offspring of Divine Mind, why are we not naturally conscious of its presence? The answer to this is: In using the privilege of our inheritance—the power to make ideas visible as things—we have created a realm that separated us in consciousness from the Father-Mind. This is the teaching of Jesus in the parable of the prodigal son. When we are weary of the sense consciousness, we have only to turn

our face (intelligence) toward our Father's house; there we shall meet a loving welcome.[7]

If you replace the word "Father" with "The Invisible" or "Infinite Self," you can see how Charles used concepts from Plato and the ancient Vedas as a lens through which to view a traditional biblical story.

The Fillmores' small Affirmative Prayer group began to grow into a multi-pronged organization with classes, an expansive spiritual publication business, and a prayer ministry that served people requesting prayer from around the world. Their spiritual home, Unity Village, hosted other New Thought teachers (including Emma Curtis Hopkins) willing to travel to Kansas City to lecture. The Fillmores also launched a radio show to share these exciting ideas and, in 1922, Charles was one of the first "preachers" to broadcast a spiritual message.

Because of the Fillmores' tireless efforts, the concepts of New Thought spread extensively. And while they never intended for their organization to become a church, it's exactly what happened. Today, it is the largest New Thought organization in the world with more than five hundred Unity churches (or Unity Centers) mostly in North America. Although each center is part of the larger Unity organization, each is independent and has a different feel and flavor.

Religious Science (now called Centers for Spiritual Living) is the other organization with the second largest number of spiritual centers founded by spiritual explorer, Ernest Holmes. He also never intended for his movement to become a church. Like Charles Fillmore, Holmes grew up in poverty and could not afford to attend college. Yet, his natural, open-minded nature, coupled with his habit of reading voraciously, introduced him to a variety of philosophies that sparked something deep within him. Ernest and his older brother, Fenwicke, began the journey into New Thought together, both finding inspiration reading Emerson's essays. Ernest also discovered the writings of Judge Thomas Troward, and together with Emerson's writings, they made an enduring impression on him.

A gifted speaker, Ernest Holmes spoke to full houses everywhere he went. He and his brother toured America, giving talks and classes based on their unique blend of the New Thought writers and the mystics who came before them. Holmes also studied with Hopkins when she was quite advanced in years but still sharp. This intensive study opened him up to a deeper level of experiencing the Divine Whole. Fenwicke reported that Ernest had repeated mystical experiences around this time, which he called "cosmic consciousness." Perhaps it was that deep spiritual experience that informed passages such as this one in his classic textbook, *The Science of Mind*:

> God is Spirit. That is, without parts. A Universal Unity and Wholeness. God is Mind. The self-knowing Mind of God is the Spirit of God and at the same time the Spirit of man . . . The conscious mind of man is the Self-Knowingness of Spirit operating through the thought of man. Hence its creativeness.[8]

Like the New Thought pioneers who went before him, Ernest Holmes realized that this One Transcendent Whole expresses as each one of us. And, because of this, we have co-creative power that we can use intentionally as we become aware of it. Until then, we use our power unconsciously and co-create our lives by default.

Holmes finally settled in Los Angeles, amicably parting from his partner/brother, and in 1927, founded the Institute of Religious Science and Philosophy. Through this organization, he began publishing *Science of Mind* magazine, which is still in circulation and going strong. The organization now has around four hundred Centers for Spiritual Living, and the Institute certifies hundreds of practitioners and dozens of ministers each year.

In the early to mid-twentieth century, the popularity of both Unity and Religious Science began to grow. These empowering ideas took hold of the mainstream population and many more traditional ministers and personal growth leaders used bits and pieces of New Thought philosophy to create their own version of "how to live a successful life." This is, in part, where the original transformational New Thought ideas became diluted and began to lose impact.

NEW THOUGHT GOES PRIME TIME

Norman Vincent Peale began to weave elements of New Thought (although he never labeled it as such) into a conservative Christian ministry. His wildly popular book, *The Power of Positive Thinking*, was certainly influenced by the New Thought concept that "your thoughts create your experience in life." His optimistic view of humanity undoubtedly helped lift many devoted Christians out of the soul-crushing "miserable sinner" message that many congregants were made to believe. Dale Carnegie took some basic New Thought ideas in a more secular direction and used them to help people become more confident and "win friends and influence people."

While there is no doubt these two popular figures, along with many others, helped numerous people, the original idea of Oneness, and how to awaken to that Oneness, was getting lost in a sea of lessons on how to "think abundantly" in order to become more prosperous and successful. It is my opinion that these more materialistic, watered-down New Thought ideas circled back into both the larger organizations of Unity and Religious Science. The movement began to lose that consciousness Emerson spoke of so eloquently, as expressed here:

> For the soul's communication of truth is the highest event
> in nature, since it then does not give somewhat from itself,
> but it gives itself, or passes into and becomes that man
> whom it enlightens; or, in proportion to that truth he re-
> ceives, it takes him to itself.

These profound ideas of Oneness are so revolutionary that, even today, many don't hear it. Because what it really means is that we are God expressing. It means we are the Eternal One and are therefore whole, perfect, and all-sufficient. It means we are the creator of our experience and, together, we are the creators of our world. Not everyone has been comfortable with such a radical idea. And so, what we hear instead is the watered-down version that sounds like this: "Affirm your good." "Expect a miracle." "Change your thinking, change your life." "God is my co-pilot." "Utilize the power of positive thinking." "I'll see it when I believe it." Now, there is nothing wrong with those ideas. They're all good. They're all correct. But if that's all people are taught, it's not going to take them very far. It skims the surface of something truly profound that radiates from the core. That may be why individuals are not experiencing the same kind of "miraculous" healings and transformation that New Thought pioneers did back in the late 1800s. But there is a growing movement of individuals who are reaching back to those original, powerful ideas that fed into New Thought, bringing them into the light and then *evolving* them. That evolving thought is what we'll explore now.

EVOLVING CONSCIOUSNESS

Because of the times during which many of these New Thought pioneers wrote (late-nineteenth to early-twentieth centuries) the writings are, by nature, dated. The language itself is dated, and the ideas, as far-reaching and groundbreaking as they were back then, do not all necessarily reflect the thinking that has evolved over time. It's one thing to so substantially water down a powerful idea that you render it inert; it's quite another to evolve an idea, which allows that concept to blossom, to reach its full potential. Our collective consciousness has evolved, and we want to embrace that evolving thought so that *we* might reach our full potential.

Let's look at a few of these ideas that are evolving:

1.   Non-Inclusive Language. As mentioned earlier, the Transcendentalists and New Thought pioneers were early feminists, and yet they wrote in the language common for the day, which was unconsciously gender-biased. The nouns "men" and "man" referred to both men and women. Women readers had to quickly translate male-centric language in their heads in order to understand that it applied to them as well. Take this sentence from *The Science of Mind*, for example, "The conscious mind of man is the Self-Knowingness of Spirit operating through the thought of man."

When reading most spiritual and self-help literature before the mid-twentieth century, women had to perform what I call the "Ginger Rogers Move." When dancing with Fred Astaire, Rogers did the same steps, only backward and while in heels! If you're a woman, a little fancy mental footwork is needed when you read some of this older material. Of course, contemporary spiritual authors have updated that language. That early embrace of women continues to evolve and now includes the full range of gender identities, sexual orientation, cultures, and ethnicities. We're *all* being empowered to realize our potential.

The second way gender bias was apparent in writings of the time was due to the influence of biblical language. New Thought writers and teachers frequently used male noun (Father) and pronouns (He, Him, Himself, and His) to describe God. The evolution of thought is that God has no gender, no location, and no personality. New Thought pioneers understood this, yet they often fell into the common parlance of the day. Sometimes, however, these same writers referred to God as a Power, or an Infinite Presence, or the Life Essence. When they did so, they came closer to sharing a more progressive, twenty-first century concept with their readers.

2. Myopic Christian Focus. Most New Thought pioneers had their roots in Christianity for many reasons—one being the limited choices in America at that time. There was not an abundance of Jewish synagogues, or Islamic centers, or Buddhist temples dotting the American landscape in the nineteenth century. The choice was between Christian denominations, such as Puritanism, Calvinism, Christian Baptists, and Catholicism. Quakers and Unitarians were there, too, but both were considerably more conservative than they are now.

Notably, the Transcendentalism movement began to shift that. Their whole purpose was to bring conventional ways of living into question. They questioned the authorship of the Bible and began asserting that all people could have a direct experience of the Divine, because all *are* the One expressing. Some—as Emerson, Hopkins, and the Fillmores did—read and studied Eastern texts, and you see this reflected in some of their writings. But, overall, New Thought writers centered their ideas on biblical stories and Jesus's teachings. Perhaps, at the time, in a Christian-dominated country, it was easier to find willing listeners. Maybe they correctly assumed more people could relate to a Jesus-centric theology, and have an easier time transitioning into a broader understanding of God. After all, one has to meet people where they are, or they won't likely listen at all.

Today, we are a multicultural, interfaith bunch and, in addition to passages from the New Testament, it is common and accepted to also hear sayings from the Buddha, Lao Tsu, the Dalai Lama, famous rabbis, Native American chiefs and Vedic wisdom. We are more comfortable embracing inspiration from a wide variety of faiths and spiritual texts, including those that originally inspired New Thought.

Secondly, there were many Christian mystics throughout the centuries that spoke of Oneness and who believed that "Christ" was a state of Divine Consciousness accessible to all, and not Jesus's last name. They further believed that humankind was born of original goodness, rather than original sin. These individuals included Origen of Alexandria in the second century C.E., Pseudo-Dionysius the Areopagite in the fifth century, John Scotus Erigena in the ninth century, and Meister Eckhart in the thirteenth century. Unfortunately, the profound ideas each of these mystics and teachers shared were not accepted by the mainstream Christian thinking of their day. In fact, without exception, each of these expansive thinkers were met with attack and their voices eventually silenced. Imagine if their Universalist ideas had actually shaped Christian thought, rather than the dominant voices that proclaimed humanity was born of original sin with true happiness only being found with Jesus in the next life. Imagine how the course of history would have changed! Fortunately, each of these individuals continued to speak and write outside the confines of the Church, and centuries later, their voices were heard by New Thought pioneers. Thomas Shepherd writes about Meister Eckhart in his book, *Friends in High Places.*

> Eckhart's legacy to modern mystical Christianity remains profound. He saw the world, like Erigena before him, as part of an eternal process of evolution/involution, unfolding and refolding, growth and change. He believed

the scholastics were right, that there is evidence for God in the physical world and in the realm of ideas. He took these abstract concepts and put them into practice. In this respect, he might be called the first father of practical Christianity.[9]

It was this more expansive idea of "practical Christianity" that many New Thought pioneers embraced. Today, there is a faction of New Thought known as New Thought Christianity centered almost exclusively on this more mystical and metaphysical interpretation of the Bible.

3. **Denial.** Denial, used together with affirmation, is a core idea that was developed early on in the New Thought movement. In order to heal, practitioners asserted, we must "deny" the appearance of sickness. Again, because of the influence of traditional Christianity, the terms used in those days to describe negative experiences were biblical, such as "sin" and "evil." Often, these early writings contained passages such as, "Deny the appearance of evil." Understand, however, that they had a very different definition of evil. Charles Fillmore saw evil as attachment to the world of illusion, the world of the senses, the belief in something other than God—something opposed to Oneness. He says, "Evil is a parasite. It has no permanent life of itself; its whole existence depends on the life it borrows from its parent, and when its connection with the parent is severed nothing remains." Therefore, "denying the appearance of evil" severs the connection to separation-thinking and renders it powerless.

Emma Curtis Hopkins explains the use of denial this way:

> Remember, denials mean rejecting the appearance against Good. Appearances against Good are the negative of Good. This we meet by denying the evil and proclaiming the Good. It is as if something denied the Good. We meet the lie with the Truth. We meet the appearance with reality. We meet the claim of absence with the truth of presence.[10]

Truly, we deny our good all the time. We live in a universe that is abundant, joyous, loving, creative, intelligent, and magnificent, and yet we live our lives as if these qualities have nothing to do with *us*. We too easily surrender to the "only-human" thinking of lack, limitation, sickness, and unhappiness because that's what we've agreed is *normal*—and it does seem to be our experience in this world of illusion. But illusion is an appearance, not Reality. So, the denial works to deny "appearances against Good." Then the affirmation follows. You affirm the spiritual reality of wholeness. This is a solid, spiritual concept. The problem is with the *word* "denial." The association today is one of refusing to look at reality. Images come to mind of ostriches burying their heads in the sand. Not a good association. And it was not the original intention to deny our experience, but rather to see it as temporary projection of coagulated thought. A better word to substitute for denial is "release." Try this on and see how it feels: "I release the old idea of limitation. That idea has no power over me. It has no reality in an abundant universe, and therefore, it's not a part of me. I release it." Does that have more resonance with you? We'll explore in subsequent chapters some effective ways to work with the power of release so that it reaches all levels of our being.

The other use of this concept of denial we want to evolve is the idea of denying our emotions. That *was* something New Thought pioneers promoted, believing negative feelings such as anger, fear, sadness, etc., were somehow not part of our spiritual nature. But the evolving idea is that we are multidimensional beings, and our emotional-self is an important part of who we are. We process our experience through our emotions, and it's important to allow that process—not deny it. To clarify, I'm not talking about wallowing in negativity. We certainly do not want to indulge anger, fear, or sadness, but rather, *allow* emotions to pass through. Paying attention to what our emotions might be telling us about our beliefs, in particular, is a valuable skill to develop! Emotions serve us best by revealing the core beliefs that give rise to them. We'll explore this in more depth in the next chapter.

4. **Mixed Messages.** In many original New Thought books, you will

find ideas of Oneness interwoven with concepts of duality. In one paragraph the author expresses a profound statement of Oneness. Then, further down the page, it seems the author is talking about a God outside of us. Maybe the author was gradually evolving her own consciousness of Oneness. In *Lessons in Truth*, H. Emilie Cady writes: "This is God pushing at the door of your being, as if He were saying, 'My child, let Me in; I want to give you all the good, that you may be more comfortable and happy.'" This is an inspiring thought, but clearly dualistic. She's referring to a God separate from us—within us, yes—but certainly a separate identity. Then in another section of the same book, Cady writes, "God does not give us life or love as a thing. God is life and light and love. More of Himself in our consciousness then, is what we all want, no matter what other name we may give it." That idea comes closer to the idea of Oneness. And if we replaced the word "Himself" with "Infinite Presence" that would be a tremendously empowering statement, fully evolved.

Even Charles Fillmore had reservations about using the word "God." He once said in a talk,

> Sometimes I don't like to call it God, because there comes into my mind the old idea of the primitive education of the soul about a God-like man. God is not like a man; God is omnipresent Spirit, accessible just like electricity, just like sunshine, just like air, to your mind, your thought.[11]

When reading these older books (and I highly recommend that you do), simply keep that in mind. Either New Thought authors were growing into the idea of Oneness or, more likely, they were growing their *readers* into it—gradually. Consider the era in which they were sharing these concepts. They might have been run out of town or even symbolically "burned at the stake" for proclaiming something as bold as, "I am God." "You are God." "We are God expressing." The Western World was likely not quite ready for such radical ideas, and needed to be gently brought to a more expansive understanding.

Fortunately, the collective consciousness is evolving to a point where we are more comfortable with the idea of Oneness.

Increasingly, more individuals are unafraid to boldly affirm, "I AM that I Am. What I am is God."

5. **The Focus of Prayer.** When New Thought began, the focus of Affirmative Prayer was mostly on physical healing, with the occasional prayer for increasing personal joy and prosperity. Early practitioners were amazingly successful in that endeavor. Today, the focus of Affirmative Prayer has expanded. Certainly, we still focus on creating an experience of radiant health, love, peace, and prosperity. These are our innate Divine qualities. However, in addition to realizing these qualities in our personal life, many of us are now viewing life from a broader, more global perspective. Our world is in crisis and most realize how important it is—for the survival of our planet and its inhabitants—to awaken to the idea that we are all one. Also, we are more globally connected. The suffering of refugees, racism, gun violence, terrorism, pandemics, and the effects of climate change are directly in our face. The world's pain is our pain, and we want to relieve it. More of us are embracing the Bodhisattva consciousness as we realize that none of us is truly free until we are all free. As a response, many choose a vocation, or engage in an avocation, that addresses these needs in one form or another. For many, our Affirmative Prayer and intention work involves visualizing the planet healing, and holding all people in our hearts as they open to the truth that we are all connected.

There are other areas in which these original, powerful New Thought ideas are advancing with our evolving consciousness; we'll explore them in detail in the coming chapters. The good news is that these powerful truths are rising to the surface, and this time, they appear fully evolved.

THE FUTURE OF NEW THOUGHT

The following individuals are among some of the leaders carrying these profound ancient truths into the future:

- Spiritual leader Rev. Michael Bernard Beckwith, whose spiritual community, Agape International Spiritual Center, is leading the way by joining together denominationally and culturally diverse people into one loving, unified, whole community. His message is one of Oneness and awakening to universal love. He writes in his book, *Spiritual Liberation*, "We are not here to 'save' the world, but to serve an emerging paradigm of love, connectedness, and generosity of heart."

  In a guided meditation to help us embody this understanding, Beckwith encourages us to affirm, "My field of perception is widening and my spiritual vision is increasing. I free myself from the clutches of the ego and make space for the universe to become conscious of itself as me."[12]

- Rev. Dr. Paul Hasselbeck is the former Dean of Spiritual Education and Enrichment at Unity Institute and his writings and teachings are truly mind-expanding. He excavated from the archives many of the Fillmores' original writings and believes we need to re-educate ourselves on these potent ideas. In his book, *Point of Power: Practical Metaphysics to Help You Transform Your Life and Realize Your Magnificence*, he says,

  > Each of us is innately good not because of our deeds but simply because we each are God expressing. It is because of this innate reality, this innate potential, that we can bring good forth in any situation...that we can bring divine order out of any event or situation. Not because the event or situation is Good or in Divine Order in and of itself, but because each of us is God expressing and has the potential to bring good and divine order forth from any event or situation. Each of us is a point of Power as God expressing.[13]

  This statement takes the powerful ideas of the early New Thought writers and fully evolves them. We are asked to progress in consciousness from seeing God as the Father who is always *with* us, to God as a power *within* us, to God as a presence working *through us*, to finally embracing the concept of the Infinite Divine *as us*.

Hasselbeck has also taken the common expression, "We are spiritual beings having a human experience," and rephrased it, proclaiming, "We are Spiritual Being*ness* having a human experience." While Michael Beckwith likes to say, "We are spiritual beings *transforming* human experience." I like to combine these two ideas and express it this way: "We are Spiritual Being*ness* transforming human experience." This phrase affirms our Spiritual Reality while clearly defining our purpose for being here.

- Gregg Braden is another conscious light who is examining evolving New Thought and grounding it in modern scientific thinking. He's working to bridge science, spirituality, social policy, and human potential. With five *New York Times* best-selling books, including *The Divine Matrix*, these forward-thinking ideas are reaching a wider audience. Braden writes about our creative power in *The Divine Matrix*,

  > Through the reality makers of imagination, expectation, judgment, passion and prayer, we galvanize each possibility into existence. In our beliefs about who we are, what we have and don't have, and what should and shouldn't be, we breathe life into our greatest joys as well as our darkest moments.[14]

  Braden understands that there are more factors at work in creating our experience than just our actions or our thoughts. He recognizes that all levels of our being create an energetic exchange within the Divine Matrix; which we might also call the Field of All Possibilities.

There are many others who are adding their expansive consciousness to the evolution of the original transformational New Thought ideas. Maybe you know of some. Perhaps you are one. If so, the world looks forward to hearing what you bring!

What we know is that we stand on the shoulders of those

expansive thinkers who came before us. Perhaps they were holding in *their* vision the evolution of these ideas that would be embraced by countless individuals who would transform their own lives and work to transform the world. Breathe that in. Feel that idea blossom in your heart. You are an integral part of the growth of this progressive tradition that is ever-evolving.

3

WE ARE MULTIDIMENSIONAL BEINGS

How much joy and pain each part of your body has experienced since emerging from non-existence! Each part has its own story to tell, holding in its memory the gifts of the Provider hidden in the pages of Time.

—*Rumi*

The previous two chapters presented the idea that the starting place for transforming your life is to cultivate the awareness that you are "the One" expressing in a unique, beautiful way. We're now going to explore the multidimensional spectrum through which that Oneness is experienced.

Today there's an endless number of ads for products and services that promote wellness for your spirit, mind, and body. It's a popular idea that is leading us to realize we are multidimensional beings. There's not a definite line where the body ends and the mind begins, or where the mind begins and spirit ends. It's all intertwined. It's more accurate to say we exist on a continuum of energetic vibration. We are, in fact, multilevel beings—*vibrational* beings—who exist on several levels concurrently, spanning the spectrum from the lightest, most expansive vibration, down to the densest. We want to embrace the fullness of who we are by accepting all aspects of ourselves as an integrated whole.

Our most dense, vibrational aspect is on the human level: this is our physical, egoic-thinking, emotional-self. This physical dimension in which our human-self lives is completely time and space bound. All physical life has a cycle of birth, growth, decline, and death, and our physical aspects are an integral part of that inescapable reality.

Within this physical dimension we also experience our emotional-self. This is the part of us that responds to life with fear, happiness, frustration, glee, anger, and sadness. Most of us want to embrace the positive emotions and try to avoid the "negative" ones. But, rather than something to be avoided or denied, all our emotions are actually an important part of our humanness. We need all of the emotions.

They are how we process our experience. They can also give us a clue into the subconscious beliefs we have about ourselves, and life in general. We'll explore that aspect more in a bit. For now, we want to look at how we experience our emotions.

For most of us, our emotional response is rarely directly derived from present situations. We experience our current "reality"—with all its peaks and valleys, all the challenges, and all the victories—filtered through our past experience. Our human-self becomes defined by the patterns we have developed in response to our experiences. And then we live from those filtered patterns.

For instance, if someone hurt or betrayed us in the past, we might have reacted to that painful event by closing our heart and shutting down. If so, then the next time someone comes into our life, we'll likely not respond directly because we're still reacting to our previous experience. We won't allow ourselves to feel the joy that comes from allowing love in, and the greater joy that comes from loving another, because we filter our current experience through the lens of our past pain that created a subconscious mantra: "no man can be trusted" or "no woman can be trusted." We end up restricting our present experience because we're caught in a past pattern. Actually, it's not the past event that caused the emotion; it's how we *perceived* the event. Our perception gives rise to the emotion, which causes a ripple in our vibrational field triggering a similar response the next time something similar occurs. Our emotional-self is responsible for creating most of our experience here in this physical dimension. We are wise to learn to work with it.

Our human-self is also defined by the degree to which we open to our Spiritual Self and allow that transcendent dimension to infuse our human life. That dimension of Pure Consciousness exists on the opposite end of the vibrational spectrum and is the essence of our being. It is our birthless, deathless, timeless self. It is our Eternal Self and is, by far, the largest part of who we are. Yet, for most people, it is the smallest part of their day-to-day experience. It is a rare individual who lives their life completely aware of their own and others' Divine Essence. For the majority, it comes as a momentary breakthrough of awareness. Those moments expand when we engage in spiritual practice and immerse ourselves in sacred community. For all but a few, the experience of that eternal Spiritual Reality is buried under the dense foliage of our human experience.

Ultimately, we all long to live fully from our Spiritual Self, but as long as we are here in this physical dimension, there is something for us to know, do, and embody on Earth. We cannot ignore the human-self, or "affirm it away." And yet, that is exactly what some spiritual teachings promote. "Deny the physical body with all its urges, longings and hunger," some spiritual paths advise, "and you'll find true happiness." Undoubtedly, there is wisdom there. We don't want to get trapped in our hunger, fear, and urges. They can absolutely lead us astray. Yet, we can't deny them either. Our body and emotions are part of our human experience. We can learn to temporarily transcend sensations through meditation and mindfulness practices, but we won't be fully grounded in our life if we make a habit of denying our emotions or our physical experience. We want to be in full residence in our life by embodying the breadth of our entire being.

POWERFUL EMOTIONS

Emotions of sadness, frustration, fear, and anger are all part of our human experience. When we experience them, the last thing we need to add to these emotions is judgment that says we're not "spiritually mature," or have somehow failed in our attempts to apply spiritual principles. That self-judgment feeds a false notion of not being good enough. I've coached dozens of people who were committed to a spiritual path, but who judged themselves harshly when they got "caught" in the emotions of anger or sadness. It's just another form of beating ourselves up that will only keep us stuck.

We know intellectually that positive affirmations and practicing proactive gratitude can shift how we feel and perceive our life. You may have actually experienced the power of shifting your perception and your energy from negative to positive. That can be very helpful in the short term. However, by continually denying our emotions and immediately attempting to "pivot to a more positive thought," we skip an important step that can have negative long-term repercussions.

Because we live in a time- and space-bound world ruled by an overall belief in separation, we grow up believing we are separate from our Source, separate from each other, and separate from our good. That worldview naturally causes us pain, self-doubt, anger, and fear, which lead to emotionally charged experiences. If we make a habit of stifling these strong emotions, pushing them down so others don't see them, it can cause real trouble. The emotions don't go away; they just go underground and become toxic. Unless that energy is effectively released, the pain becomes stored in our energetic body. This can create a blockage in the flow of life-energy and is, in turn, reflected in our body as a physical condition. You might mysteriously develop a sudden pounding headache, stomachache, backache, intestinal problems, or other acute ailment. If so, there's a good chance something is happening on a deeper level you have not acknowledged. Over time, if you continually deny your emotions, they can contribute to even more suffering—perhaps manifesting as a chronic physical condition, or repeated patterns in your life, such as financial trouble, relationship problems, and job/career issues. Refusing to acknowledge emotions very often fuels passive-aggressive behavior.

Emotions are energy and need to be released energetically. Think back to the last time you were really angry. There was a lot of energy being generated from that emotion, wasn't there? What happens to your body when you swallow that intense energy? Trying to "think a more positive thought" doesn't release the energy; that toxic energy just buries deeper in our cells.

In 2006, I was diagnosed with breast cancer. Like any diagnosis such as this, it came as a shock, particularly since I'd always taken really good care of my body. Still, deep down, I knew it was a distinct possibility. My mother died of breast cancer. In addition, as part of the fertility treatments I undertook to become pregnant, I consumed huge amounts of estrogen over the course of four years. While those two things combined were contributing factors to developing breast cancer at an early age, I knew instinctually there was more. With an awareness of being more than just a physical body, I needed to look at my condition from a more holistic view-point. I knew then that the thoughts and beliefs we harbor, along with all the ways we process our experience, contribute to our health and well-being. So I began to look deeper. It didn't take me long to discover that I had been holding a lot of resentment toward my husband for several years. I felt he was not helping me with our twin girls as much as he should, and he was less interested in my efforts to build a home-based business that focused on caring for and supporting new moms. Those resentments grew, and when I didn't feel that my issues were heard, I shoved those resentments deep inside. That's never a good place for resentments to hide.

After this realization, I had to own it. I had to acknowledge and accept, without judgment, the feelings I experienced. Then, I needed to release those emotions as best I knew how. When alone in my car, I released the anger by screaming as loud as I could, or I'd put on loud, rhythmic music and dance with abandon. Another favorite was putting on the song *Shout* by the band Tears for Fears and singing from my gut. I needed to repeat this quite a few times.

Once the energy was released from my vibrational body, I knew I then needed to work on forgiveness. I understood deep down that this was key in my recovery. I had to forgive my husband com-pletely—not an easy thing to do when you're certain you're right and the other person is wrong. Fortunately, I knew the key to forgive-ness was to separate the person from their actions. The next step is to understand and affirm that everyone does the best they possibly can with the consciousness they have at the time. Also, forgiveness is never a "one and done" activity. It's something that must be re-peated over and over. I began the process in earnest.

As a result, I felt freer than I had ever felt in my marriage. An amazing thing happens when you truly forgive: the dynamic in the relationship changes. Because I no longer intentionally gathered fuel for my resentment, I saw it less. In fact, I began to see all the ways he supported my efforts in my business, as well as his co-parenting contributions. Though small, they were still significant and very much appreciated. Truly, the more we appreciate some-thing, the more it appreciates. In addition, I cherished his loving support during my cancer treatments.

I embraced countless blessings from this experience. Not only did I recover quickly (and I remain cancer-free), but I also had the opportunity to do some important internal work that cleared out buried emotions and healed toxic perceptions. My life literally changed as a result of this experience.

Painful physical conditions and repeated patterns continually send us signals that our emotions, and the beliefs behind them, yearn to be addressed and released. They're trying their damnedest to get our attention because there's a lesson in that experience for us. In fact, pain can serve as the perfect doorway through which we encounter healing. Unfortunately, most ignore the message their pain is trying to convey and instead try to treat the pain. Or, worse, they deny it exists at all.

Because we are designed to process our experience through our emotions, it's important to allow that process to work and not deny it. Now, I want to clarify that I'm not talking about wallowing in our pain. We definitely do not want to indulge our anger, fear or sadness. But we do want to *allow* these emotions. If we acknowledge what we're feeling, *and are present to it,* it will actually pass through pretty quickly. A good cry is cleansing. Yelling or screaming into a pillow a few times with gusto releases anxiety. Taking a kickboxing class, or hitting a punching bag with a sense of purpose can release frustration.

I learn a great deal from watching my dogs' behavior. Often, after they have a tense encounter with each other, or are frustrated in their attempts to chase a squirrel, they literally "shake it off." Their entire body shakes, from their nose to the tip of their tail, as if they're wet and attempting to dry themselves. But it's not a physical sensation they're trying to shake off. It's emotional. Shaking it off releases the tension, enabling them to calm down and recalibrate.

Some time ago, I had a conversation with my daughter who is studying musical theater. I asked if she got the part for which she had just auditioned. It was a show she really wanted to do, and it seemed tailor-made for her. She said, "No, Mom, I didn't get it." I replied, "Oh, honey, how are you handling this so well? You don't seem very upset about it." She explained that, indeed, she was upset initially, and then her acting teacher taught her a technique for releasing disappointment and frustration. The idea was to get down on the ground on all fours and practice the cat/cow yoga pose (this is where you curve your back like a cow, then alternate that by rounding the back like a scared cat). Once my daughter had the cat/cow movement going, she added sounds, allowing her feelings to come up and out of her mouth in an open "ahhhhh." Apparently, it did the trick. She was able to quickly clear out her anger, sadness, and frustration. From this point on, she was free to learn whatever lesson she needed, make adjustments, and work on the next audition, released from any lingering frustration that may have led to falsely perceiving herself as a failure.

Because our emotional body is so closely intertwined with the physical, releasing strong emotions works to cleans the body, free the mind, and purify the soul.

ENERGY RELEASE

A really good shaman can intuitively feel the area in a client's body where unaddressed negative energy has become stuck. The act of energetically releasing it can involve intense deep breathing, shaking, or vocalization—both on the part of the shaman and the client. After the session, the client very often walks away free of the malady. From that point on, the responsibility for staying free of any recurrence is up to the client. They must change their underlying thinking and behavior that led to the stuck energy, or else it will return.

My intuitive sense tells me this is what Jesus did when He healed blind men, lepers, and the disabled. He didn't just say, "Pick up your bed and walk," and they were suddenly healed. His healing involved some deep mojo. I believe He was a master shaman, fully experienced in energetic healing, able to align all levels of His being with the healing power moving through and as Him. But, again, after Jesus performed the healing, the responsibility was then on the one receiving the healing, to whom He said, "Go and sin no more." In other words, you need to change your thinking to reflect the Spiritual reality of you, and not the fearful perceptions based on an egoic belief in separation. If you do, you'll be free of the malady. If not, all bets are off.

Once the energy is released, we can move back to center and feel our wholeness. From that place, we can more easily open to the love that's available, receive the wisdom that is waiting for us and feel our way into the awareness that all is in Divine Order.

Myrtle Fillmore once wrote a letter to someone requesting prayer. She confessed that she too had experienced being stuck. Her affirmations and prayers just weren't working. Then she decided to turn within and ask the Divine within her to reveal what she needed to know. She wrote:

> Spirit spoke to me very clearly, saying, 'You have looked among your faults; now, suppose you look among your virtues.' And I did; and there I found the cause of the deep-seated physical suffering and congestion! I had considered it a virtue to control my feelings; to never give way to them, outwardly; to never let anyone know when I was hurt or angered. I kept a calm and pleasant exterior, but inside I sometimes grieved and resented and worried and rebelled. And, my secret thoughts and feelings were cutting and congesting and weakening my vital organs and the wall of my body. As I turned the light of Spirit upon these hidden things and sought to have Divine Mind transform my very subconscious, so that I should work from an entirely new basis, I was healed and restored to harmony.[1]

It is also helpful to separate our emotions from who we are. In other words, it's not *my* anger; it's just anger. *I* am not angry. That's not who I am. I am *feeling* anger. It's not *my* sadness that's coming up again; it's just sadness. *I* am not sad. I am *feeling* sadness. When we refuse to identify with our emotions, we'll have an easier time letting them be, and letting them pass through.

THE GIFT OF EMOTIONS

As I indicated earlier, perhaps the greatest gift our emotions can give us is by revealing the beliefs that lie underneath them. Seen in this light, emotions are helpful tools that can point to where our thinking may be out of alignment with the highest truth of our being. Then, when we see the false beliefs, we can address them. What we can't see, we can't heal.

For example, let's say I have a constant feeling of fear in the pit of my stomach every time I get up to speak in front of an audience. If I just repeat an affirmation such as, "I am peaceful, calm and confident," I might calm those feelings temporarily, but I'll never get to what's causing them to arise in the first place. If, instead, I can *lean into* that fear for a moment and explore what that's about, I might discover I've been operating out of the false notion that, when I speak, it's the little "ego me" speaking, and it's saying, "Gee, I hope they like me, because if they don't then I have no value."

Once I recognized there is something in my consciousness fueling that emotion, I can then release the fear energetically. Remember, we are energetic beings and emotions are energy—they must be released energetically. So, I'll do something like exhale with an audible sigh, "ooohhh-ahhhh." Or, maybe I'll just shake my body, mimicking my dogs.

Afterward, I can return to my center and I'll find it easier to open to the love that's present. I can then become aware that when I allow the largest part of me to express, there is nothing to fear. That largest part of me is connecting with everyone in that audience. When I allow my awareness to open, there is a dance of Spirit between the audience and me, uplifting and awakening everyone to greater possibilities. Recognizing the fear pitted in my stomach alerts me that my thinking is off; and only after I release the energy of the emotion, can I then connect with the wisdom at my core and readjust my thinking. When I embrace this lesson, not only does it free me to be my best self, but it becomes a blessing for everyone present as well.

One of my former clients experienced an immense amount of sadness. She had a deep belief that no one really cared about her, the world had forgotten about her, and she was unlovable as she was. She would repeat an affirmation such as, "I have an abundance of friends." But affirmations didn't reach the beliefs stuck in her energetic body. The interesting part of this is that she always put on a happy face in public. She was cheerful and most people thought she was a delight. But privately, she felt very alone and the unacknowledged sadness was paralyzing her. She didn't understand why she had no energy for social activities. The effect was that she was isolating herself even further. When she tried to force herself to attend social situations, she did so with an unconscious energy of desperation, which made it difficult for others to get really close. We worked on recognizing the enormous sadness within her, and I had her do exercises that effectively released those strong emotions.

After appropriately allowing the feelings of sadness to be recognized and then released, she was able to realign herself back to her spiritual center. Once there, she could begin to see that she had been viewing herself as separate, different, damaged, and unlovable. With some spiritual guidance she began to realize that she was, in fact, connected on a deep level with everyone. She saw the commonality of all beings as we each make our way through life on our unique path. She opened to the truth that she was an expression of Infinite Love, and her uniqueness made her that much more interesting. As she began to align with that Power of Love within her, she gradually began to love herself. She was then able to genuinely radiate that love out from her heart toward others who began to feel her love and wanted to be around her. When this realization became solid, she felt ready to jump back fully into life. She is now surrounded with friends. But more importantly, when she is alone, she no longer feels lonely. She cherishes her "alone time" and uses it to nourish herself emotionally and spiritually. Now when that old feeling of sadness pops up, she recognizes it as a clue that she needs to release the tears, reconnect with her spiritual center, and readjust her thinking.

Another client came to me for some coaching around a relationship with his former girlfriend. Although the relationship had ended well over three years ago, Jim was still heartbroken and angry. He just couldn't fathom how she could have betrayed him so cruelly. He was also having trouble sleeping and experiencing stomach pain. Because he was on a spiritual path, he knew he needed to forgive her, but just couldn't bring himself to do it. When Jim felt anger, he pulled out his favorite affirmation and attempted to rise above the emotion.

Both of those actions are positive, potentially healing activities. But he was missing a very important step. He was doing what's known as a "spiritual bypass." Jim's inability to forgive her was a clear indication that he had not first owned his emotions. His sleeplessness and stomach trouble were further indications that his anger was truly eating him up inside.

Rather than trying to immediately pivot to a more positive thought, I worked with Jim on identifying the emotion when it came up, and then choosing to be present to it. We worked on techniques for releasing the energy of anger from his body. As he was an avid tennis player, I recommended that the next time he felt anger, he should grab his tennis racket and go hit some balls against the back wall of the tennis court. I asked him to be conscious of the energy as it was moving through him and to check in with his feelings after a half hour of hitting. Then, I said, "When you feel complete, take a few minutes, sit down, and take some slow deep breaths. Bring your awareness to your Inner Wisdom at your heart center, and see what it might reveal. That anger has a message for you. It's an indication of a false core belief about yourself. To discover what this is, you could ask questions such as, 'What is giving rise to this anger? Do I believe I'm a victim? Or, do I know that I am a powerful creator? How did I play a part in that situation with my ex? Do I believe I'm unworthy of love? What do I believe about the universe in which I live?'" I shared with him how it might be helpful to start keeping a journal and write down what he receives during these times of reflection.

"Only after this feels complete," I told him, "can you then repeat your affirmation that reminds you of what you know in your heart to be true. Feel your way into the awareness of Infinite Love.

Remember that you are Love Itself expressing, and therefore worthy of an abundance of love. The more you value and appreciate yourself, the more others will do the same."

We then worked together on the forgiveness exercise (which I outline in Chapter Five). After a few days, Jim was finally able to truly forgive his ex and move on with his life. I'm happy to report that he is sleeping better, his stomach issues have resolved, and he's dating again. More importantly, he embraced self-love and learned a valuable tool that will serve him for life.

Very often, the places we feel we're stuck in our lives—the places we experience pain—have embedded within them the very thing that can set us free. Rumi suggests they can reveal a story that, once understood, can propel us into our highest growth. Rather than resisting our emotions, pain, and current challenges, if we can instead learn to lean into them, we will open the door to healing and take back our power.

Now it's your turn. What "negative" emotions have you been denying, pushing down, or "affirming away?" Where are the ongoing challenges in your life that cause you pain? How can that pain serve as a doorway to your freedom?

In the following exercise, you will have an opportunity to uncover any buried emotions that may be showing up in your life as chronic physical conditions, patterns of limitation, or an inability to move forward. More importantly, you'll discover the beliefs that lie beneath them, so that you can begin the work of shifting those beliefs, which will transform your experience.

BRIEF MEDITATION

Find a place where you can sit and relax undisturbed for about 15 minutes. Allow your body to begin to let go. Start some slow, deep breaths. Allow the breath to touch every part of your body, relaxing each muscle as it flows through you. Release your thinking mind. Once you feel relaxed, consciously invite a higher wisdom to awaken within you. It will respond to your sincere invitation.

Connecting with that Inner Wisdom, start to take a mental inventory of the emotions you are most familiar with. What emotions do you frequently experience? What's on your "favorite emotions play list"? Scan the last week and see where these emotions may have come up. Are you more familiar with sadness? Sadness can take the form of discouragement, depression, grief, or hopelessness. Is anger or frustration on your frequent play list? What about fear? Fear can appear in many forms, sometimes looking like hesitation, low energy, hypervigilance, procrastination, jealousy, criticism, or even aggression toward others. When life is not going smoothly, when things don't turn out as expected and others are not behaving the way you would like them to, what emotion tends to come up for you? How long have you been familiar with this emotion?

When an answer begins to emerge, write it down in the space below or in your personal journal. Often the process of writing provides clarification.

_____

_____

_____

_____

_____

_____

Now that you have identified those frequent emotions, let's find a technique that works for you to release them. I encourage you to try each of the exercises below and then choose your favorite. At the end of each one you'll be directed to finish with the Recalibration Step.

LESSON THREE, EXERCISE ONE:
RELEASING STRONG EMOTIONS

CAT/COW/AHHHHHH

For this exercise you'll need to get down on the floor on your hands and knees. Your hands should be aligned with your shoulders, and your knees aligned with your hips. Flatten your back like a tabletop. Take a slow deep breath in and round your back as a scared cat might do. Now, slowly exhale through your open mouth while you curve your back in the opposite direction. Breathe out completely. Repeat this cycle a few times until you feel comfortable with the movement—breathing in as you round your back and exhaling through your open mouth as you curve your back. Then, once the movement feels more natural, begin to add sound to the outbreath as you curve your back. Try it first with an open, audible sigh, "ahhhhhh." Then feel free to allow that sound to be anything it wants to be. Invite the emotions of sadness, frustration, and anger you've been trying to avoid, and then release them through sound.

Play with this movement, changing it up in any way that feels natural to you. If sadness is moving through and you feel yourself collapsing in a heap of tears on the floor, go with it. If it's anger and you feel the sound becoming a scream, let it happen. The point is that the movement loosens these emotions that have been trapped in your body and begins to release them in whatever way they need to be released. Don't be afraid of the intensity. It will pass. Again, you don't want those strong emotions to remain in your body. Let them come up and let them go. When you feel complete, begin to breath naturally. Come back to a comfortable seated position and bring your attention to your heart center. Feel the spaciousness that is present now and move on to the last step of **Recalibration**.

DEEP BREATHING/VOCALIZING

This exercise is similar to the one above, with the exception of the body movement.

Stand up and allow your body to relax, hands at your side. Start taking deep breaths. Breathe deeply enough so that you can hear your breath going in and out. Continue this for a minute or two. As you continue breathing like this, allow the emotion that is most present to come into your awareness. Begin to make the breath audible with an "ahhhhhh" sound. Repeat the "ahhhhh" with each exhalation. Allow the emotion to come through sound. Don't be surprised if the emotion changes. It might start out as anger then transform into sadness or even laughter. Try not to judge. Allow your whole body to express the emotion. Stay with this exercise, allowing the emotions to come up and move out through the sound. When it feels complete, begin to breathe naturally and sit down. Move to the next step of **Recalibration**.

SHAKE IT OFF/DANCE IT OUT

You can do this exercise anytime you feel strong emotion. Just like a dog shakes off a tense moment, we humans can benefit from the same movement. Stand up and allow your body to shake, like you were wet and trying to dry off without a towel. Shake from your head, down through your torso and arms, and down into your legs. Feel the tension of the emotion wicking off your body like drops of water. Adding an audible sigh to this can be very helpful. Try it.

Alternatively, you can dance it off. Put on your favorite upbeat music and let yourself go. Dance with abandon, as you allow the emotions within you to be released through your body. When you feel complete, move to the next step of **Recalibration**.

RECALIBRATION

Now that the destructive energy has been cleared out, an opening has been created within you. Lean into this opening. Breathe into that open space in your heart and know that your breath is the One Divine Life breathing through and as you. It is the one Breath of Life breathing through and as all of creation. You are connected with the whole of Life. The qualities of this One Life are love, peace, joy, wholeness, wisdom, creativity, and abundance. Which of these qualities speak to you? Once you identify that quality, breathe it in and allow it to permeate your entire being. It's not outside of you. You don't need to "get" anything. Know that love is what you are. Peace is what you are. Joy is what you are. Infinite intelligence is what you are. This is your essential nature, waiting for you to open to it and allow that wholeness to blossom within you and fully emerge in your life.

Inherent within this sacred space, wisdom resides. Open to it now. Ask that Inner Wisdom to reveal the thinking that may be fueling the emotion you just released. Explore with your Inner Wisdom any areas where your thinking may be out of alignment with the truth of your being. Scan your consciousness for any resentment, guilt, shame, blame, or separation thinking. In other words, where do you feel you are separate from Source, from others, or from your good? What story have you been telling yourself?

Once something begins to emerge, write it down in the space below.

_____

_____

_____

_____

_____

_____

Now, take some time and investigate that thinking. Explore the story you've told yourself. Is it really true? Can you consider the possibility that it's not true after all? Survey how your experience is reflected in those stories. Notice how this old story is in opposition to truth of your being. What is the truth? Can you open to the truth that you are a beautiful emanation of the Infinite? Can you see that is true for everyone else as well? Consider how the entire universe supports your every effort to express the fullness of your being. A seed-idea of greatness is coded in your soul and the universe is set up to bring that to fruition. If your thinking does not reflect this truth, then it's time to gently bring it back into alignment.

In the space below, write a sentence or two that reflects this Higher Truth.

_____

_____

_____

_____

_____

_____

_____

_____

Now, whenever that familiar emotion arises within you again, you will know what to do.

1. Acknowledge the emotion. Instead of denying it, begin to lean into it.

2. Release the emotion energetically with one of the exercises listed above.

3. Once the emotion is completely released, return to your center. Connect with your heart-center and feel the love that is waiting for you.

4. Remind yourself of the old story you've been telling yourself,

that "out-of-alignment thinking" you identified as possibly fueling the emotion.

5. Correct your thinking. Affirm the truth of your being you wrote in the space above.

By doing these steps on a regular basis, you are ensuring that toxic emotions will never be stored in your physical body and become problematic. Instead, they will serve as the key that opens the door to your freedom, and to the realization of your Highest Potential.

Next we will explore another aspect that has the potential to sabotage our peace and fulfillment. We will meet it head on and effectively transform it.

4

THE SHADOWY FRIEND

Everyone carries a shadow . . . at all counts, it forms an unconscious snag thwarting our most well-meaning intentions.

—Carl Jung

Have you ever noticed that when you set your intention to grow spiritually, stay centered in peace, and express the loving self you truly are, everything *unlike* peace, love, and spiritual maturity is suddenly activated? Indeed, it seems that as soon as we commit to a spiritual practice, all those places in us that feel inadequate, unlovable, angry, or powerless tend to surface. Why is that? Charles Fillmore identified this phenomenon, and called it "chemicalization." He explains,

> A condition in the mind that is brought about by the conflict that takes place when a high spiritual realization contacts an old error state of consciousness . . . whenever a new spiritual idea is introduced into the mind, some negative belief is disturbed . . . and it resists.[1]

Chemicalization reminds me of detoxing. If you've ever committed to doing a "cleanse"—either fasting completely or eating only pure, live foods—your body reacts weirdly. You may feel tired, your intestines rebel, or maybe your skin breaks out. I remember giving myself facial masks when I was a teenager to purify my skin. Invariably my skin broke out in a rash of pimples the next day. The very thing I was trying to get rid of! I wondered why I bothered. What really happened was that impurities, buried deep under several layers of skin, were pulled to the surface to be released.

A similar phenomenon occurs with spiritual growth. We have a powerful "aha" moment, or a transformational experience of Oneness with the Divine, and we think, "That's it! My entire life will now be forever changed." Maybe, for a while, we experience riding that epiphany wave. But before too long, all those unacknowledged shadows that are buried within us—all the seeming "impurities," if you will—gravitate to the surface. As we explored in the last chapter, it feels to us as if someone else is making us angry, or frustrated, or sad. But, in reality, others simply trigger the angry, frustrated, and sad places within us. It *appears* that a situation in our lives is causing fear, inadequacy, or is disempowering us. In actuality, certain situations trigger the inadequate, fearful, and disempowered places within us. They're already there. They're just being brought to the surface.

When we encounter those things that provoke a reaction from us, we can think of them as bears on our path. These "bears" won't kill us, but they'll push us back. They will stop us in our tracks. They will trigger our fear, anger, frustration, shame, feelings of overwhelm, or feelings of hopelessness. Let's be clear: *No one can make you feel anything.* It is you who experiences it. And you feel it because a part of yourself that's usually repressed has been activated and is crying out. Old patterns we thought we had vanquished have only been silenced for a time. With the right trigger, they reactivate.

Until we acknowledge those places within us, and address them, our old patterns will continue to unconsciously drive our behavior. The bear wins. That may look like wanting to hide, shutting down, blaming or attacking others, lying, indulging our bad habits, finding excuses, giving up, or otherwise sabotaging our efforts to grow. We can't achieve self-mastery if we don't know what's triggering us. So, let's dive in and see what there is to explore.

As higher consciousness is awakened within us, all those places that have been hiding in the shadows are exposed to the light. What we've been repressing has suddenly awakened, and it's fighting for acknowledgement. These "shadows" will continue to sabotage our efforts until we're willing to see them for what they are . . . parts of ourselves we've disowned. They'll keep showing up—sometimes loudly—to try and get our attention. They seem to be saying, "Here I am, deal with me!" That inner "wild child" we've rejected is having its own way, acting out the way a child would if you were to ignore her, reject her, or disown her.

And if we fight back by trying to silence the shadows, or outright deny their existence, they rebel with vigor. Here's a radical idea: What if we greeted them with open arms? What if we allowed the light of awareness to shine on these shadows . . . *and embraced them*? Our personal and spiritual growth does not need to be sabotaged by our shadow. If we acknowledge and embrace these rejected places within us, their toxic energy can be released and we become whole. Think of it as spiritual detoxification.

I know that this idea of a "shadow self" can seem out of step with New Thought understanding. If we are Divine Beings . . . expressions of the One Power and Presence . . . then where is this shadow exactly? How could a separate "negative" self be created, let alone one we're not even conscious of?

The truth is, it's not a separate self. As difficult as it is to believe, our shadow self is genuinely part of who we are. We grew up in world that judged these "negative" aspects as "bad" and we were encouraged to repress them. Our parents, teachers, and authority figures scolded us for behaving selfishly, stupidly, fearfully, or when we were greedy, petulant, difficult or controlling. Some families discouraged male children from showing their sensitive, weak, whiney, childish, or vulnerable side. Girls were discouraged from showing any bossy, bitchy, selfish, or domineering qualities. And, in order to be loved and accepted (our basic human need), we forced these parts of ourselves underground.

And if parental disapproval didn't send these rejected parts of us into the shadows, then certainly stepping onto a spiritual path will. When we become self-aware, there are parts of ourselves that are no longer acceptable to us and we cannot let others see. In particular, if our idea of being "spiritual" is to be peaceful, loving, selfless, generous, compassionate, relaxed, yet focused and disciplined, then *we will deny and quickly repress* any part of us that doesn't look like that.

As we discussed in the last chapter, pushing something down so others can't see doesn't make it go away, it just goes underground. And that's where it causes trouble.

But, how do you know that a shadow self is operating in you if you've been denying it for so long?

One way to discover the shadow is to pay attention to the "bears"— the things that trigger your fear, anger, embarrassment, frustration, righteous indignation, etc. Any time you notice you are reacting strongly to something, or fiercely defending a position you've taken, there's a chance a shadow self is piping up. Or, if you ever catch yourself saying, "I can't believe I just said that," then perhaps you try to rationalize why you did something you usually don't do—you can bet your shadow self has just made an unexpected appearance.

We cannot heal what we don't acknowledge. Rather than resisting, being embarrassed by, or denying those parts of ourselves, we could choose to treat these triggers as an opportunity to understand what's unconsciously running us.

For example, I am, for the most part, a relatively caring and loving person. I think most people know me that way. But when I'm behind the wheel and stuck in traffic that's not moving, I turn into a different person. My angry, impatient, bitchy shadow gets triggered and starts running the show. I get extremely tense, yell, and sometimes even gesture. When I came face-to-face with this shadow and endeavored to discover what was going on, it became clear that deep fear was being triggered. My shadow self was afraid that I'd be late to wherever I was headed and people would think less of me. Because my shadow's name is Incompetence and Lack, this self is naturally afraid that I won't look competent and together. It raises a fear of running out of time—a deep belief that there just isn't enough time to do what I need or want to do. This same shadow self often prevents me from relaxing, and being present in the now moment and enjoying life. I always feel like I need to be moving, going, and doing. If I don't, I fear I'll get behind.

Now that this shadow self has been uncovered, I am aware of the feelings of anxiousness or anger that occasionally arise when I'm in stopped traffic. More importantly, I'm aware of what's fueling that anxiety so I can take a moment and release tension through the breath. I can then tell my shadow that I hear its fear and reassure it, like a scared child, that everything is okay. I remind myself of the gifts this particular shadow self brings (which we'll get to in a minute), and I begin to relax. As a result, this shadow self no longer runs the show or sabotages my enjoyment of life.

Another way to recognize the shadow self is to identify what you dislike in others. What drives you up the wall about someone else? What kind of behavior do you react to strongly? That's a clue this same shadow is deeply buried within you. And because you've repressed that part for so long and can't bring yourself to see it, you will project that same quality onto others. If you find yourself surrounded by people who are displaying a quality that irritates the heck out of you, you can be sure it's a deeply hidden shadow self, and you are attracting people with that same quality so you can recognize it and heal it within yourself.

In your day-to-day life, do you typically deal with unhelpful or selfish individuals? Are there people in your life who engage in gossip, have no integrity, or never do what they say they'll do? Do you find yourself surrounded by others who lie or are generally deceitful? Are you too often running into people who are excessively materialistic, shallow, or undisciplined? Do these qualities cause a strong reaction in you? As difficult as it is to accept, that's a good indication the same qualities are deeply buried within you, looking to be acknowledged and accepted. When you open your heart and bring these hidden qualities into the healing light, you'll find those people will go away, change, or just not bother you anymore.

In her book, *The Dark Side of the Light Chasers*, Debbie Ford talks about how we project our shadow onto others. She explains,

> If we deny or are uncomfortable with our anger, we will attract angry people into our lives. We will suppress our own angry feelings and judge people whom we see as angry. Since we lie to ourselves about our own internal feelings the only way we can find them is to see them in others. Other people mirror back our hidden emotions and feelings, which allows us to recognize and reclaim them.[2]

What's more, in order to prove to ourselves that *we* do not possess that "negative" quality we abhor, we will work hard to develop opposite qualities as a way to overcompensate. For example, if I have a shadow whose name is Arrogance, I may be completely repulsed by someone who walks around acting like she's better than everyone else. I'd loathe this type of behavior. I can't even entertain the notion that this same shadow is within me. So, as a way to overcompensate, I've perfected the art of humility, selflessness, and caring for those less fortunate, to prove I am not arrogant. I may compliment others incessantly, resist the urge to share my opinion, be self-deprecating, or in other ways, show I'm humble. Not that there's anything wrong with appreciating and complimenting others or being humble. Those are wonderful qualities. But when it's worn like a suit to cover up the deep shadow of arrogance, it never rings true. If, for years, I've been doing such a good job hiding this shadow, I won't even recognize it's there. What I know is that I react strongly when I see others display this type of behavior. That's my clue.

This constant repression, even if it's unconscious, takes work. We're literally fighting against ourselves. It takes an enormous amount of our energy, and it's exhausting.

In his book, *Emergence,* Derek Rydall says:

> You can't heal life by repressing it, you can't have more life by rejecting it, and you can't live more fully if you're at war with it. The path to healing any form of evil or nega-tivity—inside or out—is by embracing it, seeing through the appearance to its true nature, and reintegrating its power. That's why all the great masters have taught us to "love our enemy."[3]

We want to look at those painful areas, those places within us that we've rejected because we think they're ugly and awful. We want to recognize them, shine our light on them, embrace them—and, yes, even *love them.* We might want to treat these shadows as we would a wounded child. You wouldn't reject a child who's hurting, even if he or she were throwing a temper tantrum, because you know that some sort of pain is at the root of the problematic behavior. By approaching our shadow self this way, its destructive energy can finally be released. Exposed to the light, our shadow will no longer resort to sabotaging us in the dark. Only then, we can receive the gifts it has for us. After the toxicity is released, we can reintegrate the positive elements that can serve us.

THE GIFT OF THE SHADOW

Now, you might be wondering, "What kind of gifts could a shadow self possibly provide?" Fair question.

Let's say I've been repressing a shadow self that is uber-controlling. When I'm fearful that a situation in my life is getting out of control, or someone is doing something I feel threatens an outcome for me, my "uber-controller" gets triggered. I do my best to quell this impulse, but perhaps it slips out in the heat of the moment and I end up railroading someone. Afterward, I feel really badly about it. Or, worse, I may not even admit I did this. Perhaps I've overcompensated all my life for this urge to control by developing a skill of pretending it doesn't really matter to me. The "go-with-the-flow" attitude I've worked hard to cultivate may blurt out, "Oh well, whatever." Yet deep inside, I feel unhappy, unsatisfied, and resentful.

If, however, I've been able to recognize this "uber-controller" is my shadow self, and I choose to spend time intentionally embracing it as I would a wounded child, allowing Divine Light to shine upon it, it will no longer undermine me. The harmful, destructive part of the shadow will be neutralized and its gift can be made available to me. The gift of the "uber-controller" might be to assist me in creating more structure and stability to support my creative expression. Or, it may be to empower me to speak my truth when it's necessary. That helps me balance out the flexible, positive, creative, and free-flowing nature I've worked hard to develop.

Perhaps the shadow self you've disowned is the "bad kid" who wants to rebel, refusing to be tied down or have any responsibilities. Maybe you've overcompensated by developing the skills of paying attention to the rules, making sure you play fair, and taking on enormous responsibility, possibly to the point of burnout. If you take the time to connect with your shadow self and embrace it like the wounded child it is, you effectively release the damaging aspects of the shadow and can then receive its gifts. The gifts of a "bad kid" might be to open up your creativity, or support you in being more relaxed, spontaneous, and free-spirited. This aspect of yourself can be a lovely balance with the responsible, rule-abiding skills you developed as a response.

Are you beginning to see how reconciling with your shadow self, and embracing it with love, serves a dual purpose? First, by resisting the shadow, you have developed a muscle in response that has, in effect, honed what we would think of as "positive" aspects, such as generosity, peacefulness, dedication, love, caring, compassion, team-playing, and being relaxed, centered, self-controlled, and humble. Feasibly, you've overcompensated for an inadequate shadow by cultivating sophistication, training, education, and spiritual chops. This can all be a tremendous blessing to you. But when it's in response to something you despise in yourself, it isn't sustainable—only a part of you will be present. However, if you can heal the more destructive aspects of the shadow self, that self will give you qualities that can provide you balance. As a result, you become whole and experience full aliveness.

Embracing your shadow may also strengthen your hidden qualities, such as resourcefulness, the ability to stand in your truth, and to speak up when needed. You'll be stronger at setting boundaries, pursuing your dreams, getting your needs met, cultivating self-care, and allowing more of your spontaneity and creativity to shine. Polarity is a good thing—we don't want to be unbalanced in either direction. Remember, we are multidimensional beings, and when we embrace our wholeness, we become more balanced people. As a bonus, we free up all the energy that was spent repressing the shadow, and we feel more alive. Ford explains: "Every aspect of ourselves has a gift. Every emotion and every trait we possess helps show us the way to enlightenment, to oneness."

Let's say the shadow self you've disowned is the "angry self." Maybe you witnessed the destructive power of anger at work when your dad was angry with you or your mother, and you vowed to never let that happen in your life; you've worked really hard to repress that angry self, and whenever you begin to feel anger arise within you, you stuff it down so far that it hurts. In situations that trigger this angry shadow, you either shut down, walk away from something that might be important to you, or you become passive-aggressive. Now, certainly *uncontrolled* anger can be destructive. *Unhealed* anger carries a toxic energy. But, if you were to embrace that shadow, give it the love it's crying out for, the toxic element becomes nullified. You can then receive the gift of this shadow self.

Perhaps, for you, the angry self's gift is in becoming a master at establishing boundaries and embodying a sense of inner authority.

If you own a business, or manage a team, you might channel this energy to take bold action to ensure your success. If you work in the field of social justice, that healed part of you could energize your efforts. Many well-intentioned social justice workers act from an unhealed angry shadow, and forcefully push against it; therefore, they unintentionally perpetuate the very issues they so deeply want to help change. But acting from a place of love and strength—fueled by a *healed* angry shadow—can make for a more effective human being. Once healed and integrated, this angry self balances out the peaceful, calm, and loving side you've already developed, contributing to your wholeness.

Maybe the shadow self you rejected is the "inadequate, unworthy self." Whenever a situation arises that brings your judgment, skill, or expertise into question, you feel a tinge of fear in the pit of your stomach. Instead of acknowledging this shadow, you push it down even further. Perhaps you overcompensate by trying hard to prove how capable you are, or amassed a collection of advanced degrees to prove to the world you're knowledgeable. Yet, this inadequate shadow self is still at play, undermining any promotion, raise, or more satisfying job offered to you. Taking time to acknowledge, accept, and embrace this shadow neutralizes its undermining toxicity. Then, you're ready to reintegrate its gifts, which might be humility, empathy, and compassion, or even intuition and spiritual depth. These aspects, combined with the knowledge and expertise you've developed, allow you to express the fullness of who you are.

When we are willing to acknowledge our shadow self and, with the light of our love, heal its toxic residue and defuse its sabotaging efforts, we open to the gifts our shadow offers. We can then integrate the positive aspects of this shadow self back into our lives in a healthy way, and become much more balanced individuals.

Remember, the goal is to accept and love *all* parts of ourselves . . . the fullness of who we are. That's how we allow the masterpiece within us—with all its unique characteristics—to emerge. Embracing our shadow self is an essential part of this work.

Below is an exercise designed to reveal your shadow self and open its gifts.

LESSON FOUR, EXERCISE ONE:
MEETING YOUR SHADOW SELF

For this process you can access the recorded guided meditation on my website, Breakthrough2.com/exercises (click on Lesson 4: Exercise 1).

Choose a time and location in which you are unlikely to be interrupted for a good hour. Make sure your phone is turned off.

Choose a comfortable chair, couch, or bed to sit on, and have a journal and favorite pen nearby. You might want to light a candle, or surround yourself with comforting items.

Begin to take some slow, deep breaths. Receive ten full breaths, breathing in slowly and releasing the breath even more slowly. Allow yourself to sink deeply into whatever you're sitting on. Feel your body begin to completely relax with these breaths. Allow each breath to release any tension, and relax every muscle in your body, starting with your face, then jaw, neck and shoulders, down through your chest, belly, hips and thighs, and finally releasing any tension in your legs and feet.

You should feel pretty relaxed by now.

With another deep breath, gently bring your awareness to your heart center. This is where you are connected with Infinite Love. Feel the love from this heart center begin to expand and fill your entire body, relaxing your body even further.

Now, bring your awareness to the center of your forehead where your Power of Imagination is located. Feel that power center becoming fully activated. Breathe into that center of Imagination and begin to open to limitless possibilities.

With your Power of Imagination, see yourself now standing in a beautiful garden. It's a warm, sunny day. The skies are blue and flowers are in full bloom. Maybe you hear the melodious songs of your favorite birds. Breathe in the fragrance of your favorite flowers. The bountiful trees provide plenty of shade. Breathe in the peace and harmony of your surroundings.

You notice one large tree in particular located beside a gently flowing brook. You sit on the soft, spongy clover surrounding the tree. You are comfortable and completely at ease. The warm, gentle breeze and soothing sounds of the nearby brook relax you even further. You feel at home in this environment and are completely at peace.

Just now, you catch something in the distance: A small, dark figure, seemingly walking toward you. The figure moves closer and closer toward you. You are more curious than alarmed, remaining comforted by the surrounding beauty. As it comes closer, the figure is noticeably wearing a dark, hooded robe, with the hood fully hiding the face. The figure is coming closer and is now stands directly in front of you. You rise to meet it, hoping to see a face beneath the hood, yet the face remains hidden. You are not frightened, only curious. Who is this? What does it want? You feel for this figure. It seems so lonely, so abandoned, so rejected. You want to reach out and remove the hood to see the face, but it moves out of your reach. You start to realize this figure represents your shadow self—long ignored and hidden from view.

You feel compassion for this abandoned, disowned figure, so you reach out to take its hands. Slowly, the figure holds your hands and begins to soften in your love. Gradually, carefully, your shadow self allows you to remove the hood. For the first time, you see the face. Take a moment to explore what it looks like. Ponder why it might appear this way.

You now ask the figure which of your rejected qualities it represents. Listen closely for the answer. Take a few moments to fully receive what the figure is sharing with you. Listen as this shadow self explains when it first became clear it was not accepted, and pushed down into the darkness. How old were you? Who made you feel unaccepted when these shadow qualities were expressed? What event could have contributed to the development of this shadow? Take a few moments and allow the answers to bubble up to your conscious awareness.

You now clearly understand what this shadow self represents for you, and take the figure into your arms and embrace it as you would an abandoned child. Its negative energy seems to melt in your loving embrace. Imagine Divine Light now surrounding both you and the shadow self. The healing light of Divine Love embraces you. Take a few minutes and melt into the love.

Enjoy reconnecting with this long-rejected part of yourself. Give yourself the freedom to feel your feelings. If you sense any regret for disowning this part of you for so long, express how sorry you are for doing so. You may want to ask for forgiveness. See how your shadow self reacts to this. You may want to tell your shadow self that you forgive it for sabotaging your efforts. Explore the joy and freedom as true forgiveness blossoms from all sides.

Allow Divine Light to now lift all the shame that has held this shadow self in the dark recesses of your being. The Light now dissolves any rejection that caused this shadow to "act out." It is also lifting any and all toxicity it once held. This self is now free and ready to be reintegrated into your full, multidimensional self. Take a moment to notice how your shadow is transforming. How does it appear now?

This shadow self is now ready to give you a tremendous gift. It's time to now open up and listen for what that gift might be. Listen closely as your shadow shares how its qualities can assist you in becoming more whole. Also take a moment to acknowledge the skills you have developed by resisting and repressing this shadow that will bring balance to your life. Indeed, that is the shadow's secondary gift.

Now, you might want to gently bow and thank this self for the gift it is offering you. Promise this self that it no longer needs to hide in the shadows. This newly healed self is welcome to take its proper place in the totality of your being. You welcome its power and presence fully assisting you in being whole.

Now, take a deep breath and begin to bring your awareness back into the now. Bring your focus to your body and begin to slowly stretch. Take another deep breath and gently open your eyes.

Pick up your pen, and in your journal write about your experience. In particular, write down what this shadow self looked like, how it identified itself, and everything it shared with you. Write down what it said about its gift to you.

When you open your heart and embrace those long-rejected aspects of yourself, you develop understanding and compassion. Additionally, this new perspective will help you see how the same dynamic might be operating in others. You will become better able to be patient and understanding with others, and to forgive them. In the next chapter, we will explore forgiveness work in detail. But, before we do, there's another aspect of shadow work that is equally important to explore.

THE GOLDEN SHADOW

Take a moment and think about five people you admire. Write the name of each person in a box under the heading "Person I admire" below. Now, think about why you admire them. What qualities do they each possess that you regard highly? In the boxes in the right column, list the qualities you appreciate about each person.

	Person I admire	Qualities I appreciate in this person
1.		• •
2.		• •
3.		• •

4.	•
	•
5.	•
	•

We've all had the experience of admiring someone while feeling that we absolutely could never be as smart, talented, put together, confident, chill, accomplished, successful, disciplined, or spiritually advanced as they are. Well, guess what? The same dynamic that occurs when we project our rejected "negative" shadow onto others also applies to the "positive" qualities we admire in others. This is called our Golden Shadow. We actually possess the same qualities we admire in others because we are all expressions of the same one Divine Light. But, for whatever reason, we have not been able to accept that we are as fabulous as some others. Perhaps we were taught to be humble, unassuming, and never "toot our own horn." Perhaps we learned at an early age that when we let our light shine, our friends no longer wanted to hang around us. So we hid our special gifts and shrunk back into mediocrity. We either learned to hide this part of ourselves well, or we never developed our gifts to begin with. We have, in effect, disowned the "positive" aspects of ourselves and are now projecting them onto others. When we think about these people, we are either filled with admiration or envy.

What we know for sure is that if we really admire someone, or envy them for having qualities we wish we had, we *do* actually possess those same qualities. They may be undeveloped in us, but they are there. We admire them because our Golden Shadow really wants us to accept these aspects. Our soul wants desperately to express the fullness of our magnificence.

I believe my acting background helped me embody those qualities

I had rejected and projected onto others. I went through a phase of having terrible stage fright. Before I went on stage, my body would shake and I felt as if my heart was going to jump out of my chest. The only way I made it through was by thinking of actors or performers I admired, and I willed myself to channel those qualities that made their performances so great. I metaphorically breathed the person into my being. I felt myself embody their qualities from the core of my being out to the ends of my fingertips. Not only did that get me through, but invariably someone would say to me afterward, "Wow, where did that come from?" I didn't know at the time that what I was actually doing was activating those same qualities I admired in others that were already within me. If I had known it then, I would have allowed my full magnificence to express in my actual life, not just on stage. Of course, I actually possessed these qualities; they were just buried under mountains of self-loathing. It wasn't until much later in life that I embraced these qualities and let them blossom.

But *you* don't have to wait another minute. You can reclaim the magnificent qualities of your Golden Shadow right now.

LESSON FOUR, EXERCISE TWO:
RECLAIMING YOUR GOLDEN SHADOW

To access the guided version of this exercise, go to Breakthrough2.com/ exercises and click on Lesson 4: Exercise 2

Look again at the list of qualities you admire in others. Focus on one of those qualities. Think of the person upon whom you've been projecting your shadow. Close your eyes and, once again, activate your Power of Imagination. See this admired person standing in front of you, expressing this quality. Spend a few moments taking it in. Because you are both expressions of the same one Divine Light, you are equally magnificent as the one you admire.

Now, on a deep inhale, imagine you are breathing in the quality of this person. Feel that quality embed itself deeply at your core. Continue to focus on this quality while breathing deeply. Notice that you are, in fact, activating it within you. This quality you've admired and projected onto others is in fact yours right now. It is there as the seed idea. Allow this seed quality to grow and expand within you . . . from the core of your being, all the way out into the very tips of your fingers and toes. This quality you've admired in others is now fully blossomed in you. Imagine yourself in a situation where this quality would come in handy. Imagine you are rising to the occasion, fully expressing this quality. What does that look like? What does it feel like? Completely own this quality.

Open your eyes and be present in the room. Think about ways you can develop this latent quality within you and write several ideas for doing that in the space below. For example, if you want to embrace the quality of discipline, think of ways you can develop that. Start by setting your intention to hold yourself accountable for small things like, say, washing the dishes before you go to bed. Practice that for a while. Every morning, when you wake up, congratulate yourself for having done that. Breathe in how good it feels to have a clean kitchen in the morning. Affirm to yourself, "I have such discipline." As you continue to do this, you are building up a history of success. You are exercising your "discipline muscle" and it is growing. Then, try something that might be more difficult for you.

Maybe that's meditating daily. So, set your intention to rise ten minutes earlier, and sit down to meditate for ten minutes each morning. Every time you actually carve out the time to meditate, congratulate yourself and affirm, "I have enormous discipline." It's already the Truth of you. If you admire it in others, it's there within yourself. As time goes by, this quality you had previously admired in others, fully blossoms within you.

WAYS I CAN DEVELOP THE QUALITIES I ADMIRE IN OTHERS:

1. _____

2. _____

3. _____

4. _____

5. _____

You can do this same exercise for each quality you've repressed and projected onto others.

5

FORGIVENESS GIVES TO US

We must develop and maintain the capacity to forgive. He who is devoid of the power to forgive is devoid of the power to love. There is some good in the worst of us and some evil in the best of us. When we discover this, we are less prone to hate our enemies.

—Dr. Martin Luther King Jr.

Now that you've begun to understand and accept those long-denied shadowy aspects of yourself, you have also expanded your capacity for compassion. This new perspective can help you see how the same dynamic operates in others. It can assist you in being more patient and understanding, even forgiving of others.

Learning to forgive is not something we want to do because it shows the world we're good people of faith. Rather, it is something we want to do because our personal freedom depends on it. Holding onto resentment and being unwilling to forgive others and ourselves are the biggest factors in keeping us stuck, creating not only relational difficulties, but also impacting many other areas of our lives.

You may have learned to love and accept the fullness of who you are, embodied a consciousness of oneness, released the energy of painful experiences, and reintegrated your healed shadow self. But if you are unwilling to forgive anything or anyone, the weeds of bitterness will choke off vital life energy. Not being able to forgive someone creates a toxic energy in our body, our mind and our soul. It blocks the flow of good in our lives. It kills our dreams.

The truth is our resentment doesn't affect the other person. It's never about the other person. It's about us. As the saying goes, "Clinging to resentment is like taking poison and waiting for the other person to die." But, when we learn and practice the art of forgiveness (and it is an art, not a science), it frees us from that heavy burden of resentment, and life begins to flow more abundantly.

As everyone has a different idea of what forgiveness means, I'll clarify what *I* mean by forgiveness.

What forgiveness is NOT:

- Forgiveness is not condoning someone's hurtful behavior. Forgiveness never means excusing what someone has done.
- Forgiveness is not about allowing yourself to be hurt again by that person. And, it's not an invitation to anyone acting abusively to stay with you. Forgiveness can be—and often should be—done at a distance.
- Forgiveness does not require the offender to apologize. It also does not require you to tell that person you've forgiven him or her. True forgiveness is an internal process.
- Forgiveness is not a recommendation to bury your feelings, or pretend you really weren't hurt, or pray your anger away. Actually, the first step in the forgiveness process is to own your feelings (we'll explore this process in detail a little later in this chapter).
- Forgiveness is also not a way to absolve yourself of responsibility. In everything that happens to us, including relationships, we must remember that we have played a part, however small. Searching our hearts for our conscious or unconscious participation in creating a painful experience will free us to have a healthier relationship in the future with a better understanding of ourselves.

What forgiveness IS:

- Forgiveness is a recognition that the one who offended you is a human being who has temporarily forgotten who they are. They have forgotten their oneness with Source. They may have typically acted unconsciously and, very often, from a place of their own unhealed shadow. The art of forgiveness is about doing the best you can to separate what someone has done in the past from who they truly are, and then focus on their Spiritual Self. When you do this, you return to your natural state of inner peace and open the channels for good to flow once again in your life.
- Forgiveness is a holistic practice that happens within your own consciousness, effectively releasing you from toxic patterns. It repairs wounds and heals your soul.

- Forgiveness reaffirms your oneness with all beings. It reunites you with the whole Divinely-human race. And, when you release resentment, it's not just for yourself—you are contributing to the shift in the collective unconscious, making it easier for the world to forgive. Isn't that what the world needs now, more than anything? Love, understanding and forgiveness? As the Dalai Lama once said, "Without inner peace, it is impossible to have world peace."

Now, I don't want to give you the impression that forgiveness is easy. Forgiveness can be difficult, particularly for big offenders such as those who have deeply betrayed you in one way or another. It is not easy. It's not a one-and-done exercise.

It's important to remember that forgiveness is a process. That's why Jesus told his followers to forgive "seventy times seven." I don't think he was being literal. But, rather, he knew that forgiveness is a practice. It's a practice that begins with a *willingness* to forgive. Complete forgiveness is a goal to which you move closer each time you practice. And it's a practice that reaps rich rewards. When you forgive someone, you are actually giving a gift to yourself. Your willingness to forgive opens the channels within you, which then allows the gifts of peace, joy, healing, and the realization of your dreams. Forgiveness is the key that opens the door to personal freedom.

THE PROCESS

When considering the one who hurt you, you must understand that one of three things occurred:

1. This individual had no awareness that their actions would cause another's pain. They were simply following their own path (however unenlightened you think it might be), and you simply stepped into it. It's also possible you are taking their behavior personally when it was neither intended nor malicious toward you.

2. It's possible this individual was unconsciously acting out of their disowned shadow self. As we explored in the previous chapter, a repressed shadow-self can sabotage good intentions. The unhealed shadow blocks the light of the Divine Self. Our task is to remember that shadows are created out of pain, and to see that behind and within it, there is pure love. If this person knew the love that existed inside them, and they were able to express it, they would have done so.

3. If we continue to repress and disown the shadow within *us*, we will continue to attract others who express these rejected qualities until we can see and accept it within ourselves. If you keep attracting the same kind of person who is repeating a similar pattern, you can be sure it's a message from your inner self that it's time to reclaim those qualities within yourself. When you do, you will no longer need to attract others who display those behaviors.

As human beings, we are perfectly imperfect. We all make mistakes. In some faiths this is interpreted as original sin, and one who continues to sin is known as a "sinner." The word "sin" is actually of Greek origin. It was used in archery and referred to "missing the mark." Missing the mark is not a sin—it's a mistake. A person who makes a mistake is not called a "mistaker." They're just someone who made a mistake.

The whole idea of sin has been heartbreakingly misinterpreted to imply that someone who makes mistakes is bad and therefore doesn't deserve our forgiveness . . . that only God can forgive a sinner. We need to understand that no one is inherently bad. Theologian Matthew Fox insists we are born of "original blessing." As expressions of the Divine One, we are all born innocent; when we make our way through life, we forget who we are, so we naturally make mistakes. Some, because of upbringing, or lack of self-esteem, might act in a way that we perceive as bad and impossible to forgive. It is possible to forgive anyone if we separate the true self from his or her mistakes. Again, we're not condoning the individual's behavior. Instead, we are choosing to look beyond the mistakes that arose from their fearful, separated self, and see the love at their core. Ignorance of the connection to one own's inner Divinity produces fear and shadows, which are often the unconscious motivating factors behind all destructive behavior. Therefore, all we ever need to forgive is ignorance.

RESENTMENT HURTS US

Have you ever noticed that when you hold a grudge against someone, they continue to be a problem in your life? What feelings are brought up when you think about them? Do you feel rising anger, a sinking heart, frustration, or fear? Even when you are not actively thinking about the person or situation, the anger is still there, robbing you of your peace of mind. Stored in the deep recesses of our consciousness might also exist resentment against our parents, our ancestors, a perceived enemy, a race, a political party, or group of people.

Practitioners of mind/body medicine tell us that many illnesses are caused directly by an unforgiving attitude. Animosity and rancor are toxins that poison the body temple. Even those in traditional medicine are beginning to research how our emotions, including resentment and unforgiveness, play an essential role in our mental and physical health. It has been a long time in coming though. In Jim Dincalci's book, *How to Forgive When You Can't,* he writes about why it has taken so long for psychologists to recognize the healing power of forgiveness:

> Most psychologists, Freud in particular, rejected church control and interpretation in matters of mental health . . . psychology in general rejected forgiveness because it was associated with "The Church" and its doctrine. As a result, forgiveness was lost to the professional therapy community.[1]

Fortunately, therapists are now realizing that our unwillingness to forgive only hurts ourselves, not the individual who hurt us. When we perceive that someone has wronged us, we allow a wound to develop, which festers over time. This wound hinders our ability to become whole, which, in turn, adversely affects other areas of our lives. Forgiveness heals and releases us from a poisoned body and an unfulfilled life. Mary Ann Morrissey tells us in her book, *Building Your Field of Dreams*:

> Those emotions create a tremendous void in us and around us. If you refuse to forgive, all those toxic feelings of hatred and resentment stay bottled up inside, eventually seeping into other areas of your life. The offender doesn't suffer. It is your own life, your own dreams that are stunted . . . In order to free the dream inside you, practice forgiveness every day.[2]

Every day? Yes. Again, forgiveness is a process that takes time and effort to work through. Also, if we feel we've already forgiven the big offenders in our life, we might not think we need to practice forgiveness every day, right? But little resentments accumulate over the course of a day and can get under our skin just enough to make a difference. When we don't take the time to consciously release resentments, they build up day after day, and have the cumulative effect of poisoning our body and sabotaging our success.

When we are willing to practice forgiveness it will release the free flow of well-being into our bodies and a flood of good will pour into our lives. The following passage from *A Course in Miracles* eloquently describes the power of forgiveness:

> Ask not to be forgiven, for this has already been accomplished. Ask rather to learn how to forgive. Forgive the world and you will understand that everything that God created cannot have an end and nothing he did not create is real. Do you want peace? Forgiveness offers it. Do you want happiness, a quiet mind, a certainty of purpose and a sense of worth and beauty that transcends the world? Do you want care and safety and the warmth of sure protection always? Do you want a quietness that cannot be disturbed, a gentleness that never can be hurt, a deep abiding comfort and a rest so perfect it can never be upset? All this forgiveness offers you. You who want peace can find it only by complete forgiveness. Forgive the past and

let it go, for it is gone. Lift up your eyes and look on one another in innocence born of complete forgiveness of each other's illusions. Whom you forgive is given power to forgive you your illusions. By your gift of freedom is it given unto you. Those who forgive are thus releasing themselves from illusion, while those who withhold forgiveness are binding themselves to them[3].

The power of forgiveness is truly miraculous. After you have sincerely forgiven someone, your relationship will be recreated; they'll change, you'll change, the dynamic of the relationship will change. They may gladly disappear altogether from your life, or they will simply no longer affect you. In short, you will be free.

The same principle applies to those who have either passed away, or are no longer in our lives, but still have an effect on us. A friend once said, "My mother is always criticizing me—and she's been dead for ten years." Until we forgive others we will be victims, shackled by the chains we've tied to ourselves. Let's give ourselves a break. We hold the key to personal freedom, and that is through forgiveness.

FORGIVING WHEN IT'S DIFFICULT

A dear friend, Rhonda, endured one of the worst tragedies anyone can imagine. When she was fourteen years old, she witnessed her father shoot and kill her mother, then turn the rifle on himself. In less than five minutes, this man had taken away the most important person in a child's life and left an indelible impression of violence and horror upon her developing psyche. Because she was a religious girl, she knew the only Christian thing to do was to forgive her dad—which she did to the best of her ability. Only later did she discover her act of forgiving was, understandably, superficial at best.

Her difficulties adjusting to life alone, tormented by anger and fear, began to manifest in her early twenties. She would frequently act out by drinking and manipulating men. Unable to sleep, she became anxious, depressed, and hopeless. Rhonda's pain became so unbearable she attempted suicide three times. Finally, at the age of twenty-seven, Rhonda decided that, if she were to make it in life, she would have to sincerely forgive her father—and not just give it lip service.

As she worked through deeper and more meaningful levels of love and forgiveness, she began to open to her own inner peace as well as life's possibilities. Her fear subsided as she learned to trust that she was safe in a benevolent universe. Her spirituality deepened with each passing day. Now, an Emmy-Award winner, author of the best-seller, *Fearless Living* and founder of the Fearless Living Institute, Rhonda Britten assists countless others in living successful lives.

Could anyone blame Rhonda for hating her father for his horrendous crime? Most would think she was justified in harboring tremendous, life-long resentment toward him. However, had she chosen that path, she would have continued to be a victim, leading a life of self-abuse and dysfunction. She also never would have realized the remarkable healing and blessings that were in store for her, not to mention the blessings for those she now assists.

Fortunately, most of us do not have as challenging a lesson in forgiveness as my friend. For the majority of us, forgiving someone who has broken our heart, or cheated us in a business deal, seems like a distasteful, if not impossible, task. Often, it's more difficult for us to forgive those we love because we tend to hold them to a higher standard.

Although it may be more difficult to forgive someone who has committed a violent crime, as was the case for my friend, it is possible and ultimately necessary to be able to transcend the painful experience. This doesn't mean we should not first own and be able to express our anger and grief. Actually, it is essential to the process of forgiveness to feel and process our emotions. Once all our feelings are acknowledged and released in a heathy way, the way is made clear for the cleansing, healing experience of true forgiveness.

LESSON FIVE, EXERCISE ONE: FORGIVING OTHERS

1. Using the space below, make a list of everyone you need to forgive—even those with whom you may feel only a twinge of resentment. Don't feel you need to fill up the list, but do list those who come to mind.

- _____
- _____
- _____
- _____
- _____
- _____
- _____
- _____

2. Next, use a separate piece of paper and write a letter to each person, one at a time. The letters will not be sent to the listed individuals; they're only for you. Write down everything this individual did to hurt you, how it made you feel, and how it affected your life. Allow the full spectrum of feelings to come up for you, including anger and sadness. Really be present to what you're feeling. Release your tears or scream into a pillow. Let the feelings move through you and out onto the paper.

3. After you've spent time allowing your emotions to be released, fold the piece of paper and hold it in your hands. Take a moment to connect with your heart center. Breathe into that heart space and when you're ready, say the following intention statement, replacing the words "this person" with the individual's name:

"From the awareness of my highest self, I realize that [this person] is a spiritual being having a human experience. I understand that it is natural for him/her to make mistakes while he/she is learning here on Earth. [This person] did the best he/she could with the understanding they had at the time. I do not take it personally. I now forgive [this person] for every mistake I've written here. Indeed, I am only forgiving ignorance. I will remember [this person]'s highest self, even if he/she has forgotten. I now claim a new learning, a new understanding, and a blessing from this experience."

4. Finally, burn the letter while repeating the following seven times through:

"I forgive. I release. I let go."

Proceed through your list one person at a time, working through the process completely. You may want to do this exercise all in one day, or space it out over a period of time. This exercise will feel uncomfortable. Move forward with it anyway. It's not about comfort; it's about healing.

PICTURES SPEAK LOUDER THAN WORDS

Here's another exercise that can be very helpful in the forgiveness process:

Look for an old photo of the person you'd like to forgive as a child or a very young adult. If the person you need to forgive is one of your parents, or an ex-spouse (and for many that is often the case), it should be relatively easy to locate a photo of them in their youth. If not, use the power of your imagination to invoke an image of the person as a child.

Look carefully at the photo and begin to engage in an imaginary conversation with the young person in the photo. Be open to hearing the voice of that child. Ask them what their dreams are. Ask what their fears are. Ask what it was like growing up in their family. What were the influences and pressures they encountered? You can get a lot of information from a candid photo.

You are seeing this person not as the adult who hurt you, but as a fragile, vulnerable young person. And, if you look carefully, you may begin to see a wounded spirit who was just trying to make it in a world based in separation. As all human beings do, they began to cover up their pain with defenses, coping mechanisms, and developed patterns that were counterproductive to themselves and others in their lives. Also, as you discovered in the prior chapter, because we disown the parts of ourselves we dislike, those rejected parts act out and can sabotage our relationships and our good intentions.

Take some time to focus on this vulnerable young person and begin to open your heart slowly. See if you are willing to send love to this child. Tell them you forgive them. You may also want to read the intention statement from the preceding exercise directly to the person in the photograph.

Many find this exercise very healing. It's worth every effort to find a photograph. But again, if you cannot find an old photo of the person as a child, the power of your imagination will work fine.

Charles Fillmore wrote about this miraculous power of forgiveness a century ago:

> Thus in spiritual understanding, the I AM of man forgives or "gives" Truth "for" error; the mind is set in order and the body healed. The moment man realizes this he puts himself in harmony with the Truth of Being, and the law wipes out all his transgressions.[4]

LESSON FIVE, EXERCISE ONE: FORGIVING YOURSELF

Forgiving ourselves is equally important and often more difficult to do. Some of us are harder on ourselves than we would ever be on others. And, as we've been exploring in this book, the toxins of our own harsh self-criticism are just as poisonous as our resentment toward others. Accepting the fullness of who we are—our perfectly imperfect self—is essential to realizing our dreams. Lack of self-worth often stems from an experience where we did, or did not do, something for which we feel ashamed. It could be a period of time in the past where we behaved badly. It might be for something which we're not even aware—buried in the deep recesses of our subconscious.

Maybe you're conscious of this experience, but don't give it much importance. Yet it's a toxin, infecting the realization of your good. Through this exercise you will come to terms with your past and heal all its negative influence. Then you will offer yourself the gift of self-forgiveness and complete self-acceptance.

Write a letter to yourself describing your more glaring mistakes. Some may have this information at their fingertips, while others may need to do a little more soul-searching. Examine if you have hurt someone either by your actions or lack of action. Where have you been unkind? Where could you have done better? Where have you wasted your time here on Earth? Dig deep, and then let the words flow onto the paper.

1. Allow the fullness of your emotions to be present and accept them fully. Identify your feelings. What are they? Anger? Discouragement? Disappointment? Shame? Sadness? Allow them to move through you and be released.

2. When that feels complete, take a few moments to turn within and connect with your heart center. Breathe into that space. If it feels right to you, imagine your angel, guide, guru or any unconditionally loving being holding you and loving you through this entire process. Wh   en you're ready, fold the piece of paper and hold it in your hands while saying the following intention statement:

"From the awareness of my Highest Self I realize that I am a spiritual being in process of awakening from this dream of separation. I realize that, as part of this learning process, it's natural for me to make mistakes. I absolutely did the best I could with the understanding I had at the time. Therefore, I can now forgive myself for every mistake I've written here. I forgive myself and I love myself. I claim a blessing from each situation. Truly I have learned and grown from each experience. I open to see love, to experience love, and to be Love."

3. Finally, burn the letter while you repeat the following seven times through:

"I forgive. I release. I let go. I give the gift of forgiveness to myself."

FORGIVENESS AS A WAY OF LIFE

We live in unprecedented times. It seems that our darkest collective shadows are rising to the surface. We're seeing increased judgment and outright hatred of individuals and groups different from than our own. As I write this, the world is erupting in protests in cities across the globe. America's collective shadow of racism—fed by the underlying "original sin" of slavery that was never properly addressed—is rising to the surface to be healed. Our collective shame is calling us to hear it, and see it, so we can heal it. Only then can we make real changes in policy.

Our younger generation is courageously helping to bring about change. They can no longer tolerate human rights abuses, racial bias, gender bias, or ethical lapses in their leaders. They lead the charge to expose white privilege, cis-gender privilege, neurotypical privilege, and obscene income disparity. For too long we have ignored the shadow of power. And it has cost us dearly.

Corporations deny that their actions are poisoning our planet faster than even scientists predicted. People are living in denial about the need to actually change their behavior to slow climate change. The planet our children and grandchildren will inherit is questionable at best. Our collective shadows are screaming at the top of their lungs. The unaddressed aspects of the collective unconscious are coming to the surface to be healed once and for all. It's time to hear its voice, do what we can to atone for past wrongs, and embrace each other in forgiveness.

At our core, we are all one, therefore what we do to others we are doing to ourselves—literally, not figuratively. Some call it the law of karma, or say as we did in the '60s, "What goes around comes around." It's time we remembered. If we treat others with disrespect, we will be treated reciprocally. If we cheat others, we will be cheated. If we lie to others, others will lie to us. If we judge and condemn others, we are inviting judgment and condemnation from others. Whatever we do to others will be done to us; not necessarily by that individual, but the energy will revisit us somewhere down the line. As New Thought mystic Joel Goldsmith said,

"Nobody can benefit us; nobody can harm us. It is what goes out from us that returns to bless or to condemn us. We create our own good and we create our own evil."

Even if we silently resent others, we are broadcasting unloving energy that keeps us trapped in a negative spiral. We are all deeply connected with each other and we can no longer assume that our thoughts and feelings have no effect on others or the larger world. The only way up is through. We must take a good look at how we're thinking of others and heal that thinking. Forgiveness can release us from the karmic wheel.

The world is gradually moving toward an awakening of oneness. Looking through the eyes of oneness, forgiveness becomes a method for breaking down the barriers between "self" and "other." When we come to this realization, we naturally want to treat others as we would like to be treated, because we realize they are us. We will then automatically live in integrity with one of the greatest spiritual laws in the universe.

It's no coincidence that every major religion has its own version of the Golden Rule:

Christianity: "Do unto others as you would have them do unto you."

Islam: "No one of you is a believer until he loves for his brother what he loves for himself."

Taoism: "Regard your neighbor's gain as your own gain and regard your neighbor's loss and your own loss."

Judaism: "Thou shalt love they neighbor as thyself."

Hinduism: "Men gifted with intelligence should always treat others as they wish to be treated."

Sikhism: "As Thou deemest thyself so deem others. Then shalt thou become a partner in heaven."

Buddhism: "In five ways should a brother minister to his friends and familiars—by generosity, courtesy, and benevolence, by treating them as he treats himself, and by being as good as his word."

The Golden Rule is a common thread in every major religion because it is Universal Truth. From the beginning of time, truth seekers have observed that by following this one principle we are rewarded with a life of peace and well-being. Imagine if everyone actually practiced these words. Our entire planet would transform.

LESSON FIVE, EXERCISE THREE:
DEVELOPING A FORGIVING ATTITUDE

The following exercise will assist in keeping your mind clear, your heart open, and your energy field vibrating at a high level throughout the day. With practice, this attitude will become a central part of your energetic field attracting love, kindness, and harmonious relationships. And you will be doing a large part to help heal the world's collective shadow.

- Shortly after rising, while getting ready for the day, repeat to yourself, either silently or out loud:

  "From the awareness of my Highest Self, I will do my best today to remember that I am Divine Beingness transforming human experience. I commit to remembering that I, and everyone else, am on a journey toward wholeness. I forgive myself and others of all mistakes and am grateful to know who we all truly are."

If you genuinely desire to see the authentic loving self of everyone you meet, then that is what you will see. As you now know, we are all interconnected. Others will feel your intent on a very deep level and will respond in kind. As Goethe wisely stated, "Treat people as if they were what they should be, and you help them become what they are capable of becoming."

6

UNDER THE INFLUENCE

(of the Collective Unconscious)

Darkness cannot drive out darkness; only light can do that.
Hate cannot drive out hate; only love can do that.

—Dr. Martin Luther King Jr.

A growing number of people today understand the correlation between negative, limited thinking and the limitations they experience in life. This understanding, once the domain of New Thought, is being adopted by the mainstream. Unfortunately, most people still believe all they need do to change these negative beliefs is to replace them with "positive" thoughts. They're understandably frustrated when they discover it's not as simple as that. Thus far in this book, you've learned about the deeper aspects that must be addressed to create real transformation. But there is one more thing we need to factor into the equation—something that most don't consider.

Behind the experience of being stuck, there is typically either a belief based in separation, an unresolved shadow, unexpressed emotions, unforgiveness, or lack of self-acceptance. In most cases there is a somewhat direct link between our ability, or inability, to realize a joyous and successful life and the underlying forces within our minds and hearts. That's good news because this is completely in our control. We can make the needed shifts, as have been outlined in previous chapters to release what's not working and open to the natural flow of well-being and abundant good.

Sometimes, however, there's not such a direct line. Sometimes an experience truly does seem to come out of nowhere. You can search and search your consciousness and find no correlation. You didn't grow up surrounded by that kind of thinking. It wasn't in your environment. It's not related to a shadow. Maybe you've never even considered that particular thing could happen to you.

What's going on there? Either our consciousness shapes our experience or it doesn't.

We're also left scratching our head when considering global experiences such as war, tragedies, weather disasters, babies born with severe conditions, pockets of poverty, widespread disease in certain parts of the world, and global pandemics. As I write this chapter, we are in the midst of the novel coronavirus pandemic. Our world is gripped in fear of COVID-19, and there is no solution yet, other than complete worldwide lockdown. Unless you are a virologist, or Bill Gates, or a big fan of the movie *Contagion*, you probably didn't have it in your consciousness that something like COVID-19 could have happened in such a devastating way.

We can also think of unexpected blessings such as huge lottery wins, tremendous unanticipated windfalls, spontaneous healing that one never prayed for, or places where there's sudden economic expansion, community engagement, or collective expressions of kindness. In some cases there does not seem to be direct link between what's going on in consciousness and a particular experience.

We can't always know why tragic events happen, or why an explosion of good inexplicably appears in one's life. We can't know what each soul agreed to before incarnating into this lifetime in order to evolve. What we know for sure is that there is always some good to be found in every experience we would otherwise call a tragedy. When we find it, it can change our lives. Sometimes it can change the world.

Looking at this current pandemic—while it's a heart-wrenching tragedy so many people have lost their lives or their livelihoods, still there is tremendous good emerging from this experience. It is a universal spiritual principle that old ways of being must give way in order for something greater to be birthed. In nature, we see that acorns need to break apart and give way, in order for the future oak tree within the acorn to emerge and grow into its full potential. Caterpillars must completely give up everything they know; they must entirely dissolve in order to become a butterfly. As I write this, life as we know it is currently on pause. And some things will never come back. But if that's a way of life that is not sustainable, or a way of being that is no longer working, then maybe that's a blessing. You can't build a better world on a flawed foundation. Our planet is getting a much needed to chance to breathe and restore itself. We are learning about what's truly important. We are also learning new ways of communicating with one another. Instead of being in competition with each other, scientists are working together to find effective treatments and develop a vaccine. Industry is retooling to provide what is needed for the greatest good of the whole. Countries are sharing information, resources, and best practices. The old structures of competition, hoarding, and nationalism are beginning to shake loose, and a new consciousness is growing—one of cooperation, volunteerism, community, and sharing what we have with others. This pandemic, and the effort to mitigate it, are highlighting systemic inequities and injustices in our society we can no longer ignore. It's as if an old way of life needed to die in order for something more meaningful to be born.

From our limited perspective we cannot see the full picture. We can't know why things happen that seem, on its surface, random or tragic. But that's because we're peering at life from a tiny keyhole. We can widen that keyhole by intentionally expanding our consciousness, but we'll never see the complete picture. One of the ways we may widen our view, however, is by understanding the tremendous impact of the *collective unconscious*.

Ernest Holmes wrote extensively about the influence of what he called "race-mind consciousness" (referring to the human race). Swiss psychiatrist and psychoanalyst, Carl Jung, described this phenomenon as "the collective unconscious" or "collective psyche." What both Holmes and Jung understood was that all humanity shares a collective mind, which acts as a virtual "warehouse" for all human experience, archetypes, ideas, and beliefs. And since the majority of humanity has been born into a dream of separation, ideas of lack, fear, limitation, struggle, powerlessness or domination, make up much of the content of the collective unconscious. At the same time, all the prayers, affirmations and expressions of love and compassion throughout human history are included as well. Together, this collective unconscious directly influences each individual consciousness, and in turn, expresses in our individual and collective experience.

Dr. Jung believed, more than any other factor, that the pervasive perceptions of the collective unconscious affect the experience of the collective, as well as our own. He wrote:

> Our personal psychology is just a thin skin, a ripple on the ocean of collective psychology. The powerful factor, the factor that changes our whole life, which changes the surface of our known world, which makes history, is collective psyche, and collective psyche moves according to laws entirely different from those of our consciousness.[1]

Jung certainly took this idea to the extreme. I wouldn't go quite that far, but undoubtedly there is considerable influence . . . more than we realize. Think about it: all the thoughts of humanity, all the fears, anger, judgments, resentments, and disrespect for our planet—for generations—creates a heavy vibration that is present in the thought atmosphere.

Interestingly, well before Jung posited his theory of the collective psyche, Swami Vivekananda, the spiritual master from India, expressed a similar idea. When Vivekananda appeared at the first Parliament of World Religions in 1893, he spoke of oneness consciousness. When he did, he fueled the flame of a new movement. He said:

> The whole universe is simply an ocean of matter, of which you and I are like little whirlpools. Masses of matter are coming into each whirlpool, taking the whirlpool form and coming out as matter again. The matter that is in my body may have been in yours a few years ago, or in the sun or in a plant, and so on, in a continuous state of flux. So it is with thought. It is an ocean of thought, one infinite mass, in which your mind and my mind are like whirlpools. Are you not seeing the effect now, how my thoughts are entering into yours and yours into mine? The whole of our lives is one.[2]

In our embrace of oneness consciousness, we can open to the deep beauty of this elegant truth. Spiritually speaking at our core we are all one. Additionally, we are all connected on the mental level, being expressions of this One Mind. We tend to think our mind is separate from everyone else's mind. We see it as encased in our brain. Solid. Impervious. You can't know what I'm thinking and I can't know what you're thinking. But such is not the case. We share the totality of our collective thinking, for good and for bad. Until we are aware of this collective unconscious infused with beliefs of separation, victimization and fear, it can unwittingly contribute to conditions such as illness, lack, and misfortune in our own personal world. And that is the keyword here, "awareness." When we become aware that the collective unconscious can and does influence our experience, that's when we can do something about it. Awareness is key. We can learn to consciously protect ourselves from the negative influence of this group mind, while welcoming the aspects that are beneficial to us.

COLLECTIVE CONSCIOUSNESS IN ACTION

Mary Ellen is a wonderful massage therapist and body worker. She truly has a magic touch. She seems to be in tune with whatever is going on in a patient's body, and can pinpoint with a surgeon's precision where there's tightness and stuck energy. It's because she's such an intuitive healer that she is so effective *and successful*. But being an intuitive healer also has its drawbacks. We've become friends over the years and invariably she shares with me a story of a disastrous thing that just happened to her. A tree fell during a hurricane and smashed in her roof, just barely missing the bedroom where she was sleeping. She suddenly found herself responsible for her aging mother's medical bills. Last year her identity was stolen. If you've ever had that happen, you know what a nightmare it is. That's when she decided it was time to work with me. In our sessions we explored possible relationships she may have not forgiven or was in judgment about. Nothing there. She has worked diligently to forgive everyone and is truly the most accepting person I know. Then we explored possible lack of self-acceptance. Although she still has some work to do in that area, she's made much progress. Overall, she has a positive attitude toward life and practices gratitude daily. It was puzzling. There did not seem to be a direct cause and effect. The content of her consciousness and her experience in life didn't seem to match.

I suddenly realized what might be happening. Mary Ellen's intuitive ability to read others' energy leaves her open to so much more than that one person's individual energy field. She's opening her consciousness, and her own energy field, to the influence of the collective unconscious. Certainly all of us are influenced by the collective unconscious, but when someone intentionally opens their energy field in order to "read" another, it's like opening all the doors to the vast "whirlpools" of consciousness, and leaving them wide open. Shared beliefs of disaster and misfortune abound in the collective unconscious. When she realized this, Mary Ellen was naturally concerned. "Does this mean I have to close myself off to others? I won't be able to do what I do." I reassured her she could continue to provide the same amazing service to others as she always had. She just needed to make one adjustment.

"When you begin your work, do whatever you normally do to get into a receptive state and bring yourself into oneness with your client. But, from now on, I'd like you to affirm with all the power you have as a creative being that you are opening to *only* this one person. Affirm that your consciousness is closed to the influence of the collective consciousness. If it helps, imagine a wall around your body with only one window open that is in direct connection with your client. You two are connected through that open window. Then, once you've finished your work with this client, close the window and do the clearing exercise." (described below)

Mary Ellen has been using this technique and she's having great success. After some Affirmative Prayer and forgiveness work, she was able to resolve the stolen identity issue rather quickly, without any damage to her credit.

If you think only people working in the healing industry need to be concerned with being unwittingly influenced by the effects of the collective unconscious, the truth is *everyone* is influenced by this group mind. As Vivekananda said, we are all whirlpools swirling in one Infinite Divine ocean and are not separate from each other. We are susceptible to the group mind influence at all times, but perhaps even more so during periods of relaxation, meditation, and sleep. One can also be vulnerable during periods of depression, or while under the influence of alcohol or other mind-altering substances.

Not to worry though; we can easily protect ourselves from the negative influence of the collective unconscious with the following exercise.

LESSON SIX, EXERCISE ONE: THE NET OF LIGHT

You can do this exercise before you go to sleep, before meditating, in the morning as your day begins or at any other time of the day.

Take a moment and breathe in deeply. Connect with your higher wisdom. From this place, remember that you are a powerful co-creator. You are, in fact an expression of the Creative Power of the universe.

Imagine there is a giant net surrounding you made of angelic light. Feel yourself enfolded in this angelic light. All negative, fearful, limited thinking is being caught by this Net of Light. Not one idea based in separation can get through. They burn up the moment they hit the net. The only thoughts that can get through this net from the collective unconscious are the ones you welcome—positive, loving, and transcendent ideas based in oneness.

Solidly affirm: "My energy is closed to all but Divine ideas." And know that your word as the powerful, creative being you are makes it so.

LESSON SIX, EXERCISE TWO: ENERGETIC CLEARING

If you work in any type of healing profession, or do spiritual counseling, you may want to do this exercise that I recommended to Mary Ellen.

After your client leaves, stand up and, using your hands as brooms, work from the top of your head down to your feet shaking off the energy as if you were sweeping through your vibrational field. Brush away any negative energy. Breathe deeply throughout, exhaling audibly through your mouth.

Again, visualize a Net of Light surrounding you and affirm, "My energy is closed to all but Divine ideas."

GENERATIONAL INFLUENCE

Nowhere does the collective unconscious influence us greater than from our own family tree. Again, for good and for bad. Generational influence is just as powerful as genetically inherited physical traits. We unwittingly inherit our ancestors' fears, bigotry, victimization, and trauma, along with an endless variety of false core beliefs based in separation. On the other hand, we may have also inherited their strength, tenacity, innate healing wisdom, compassion, and ability to triumph over tough circumstances.

Think for a moment about your parents, their parents, and their parents. Some Native American tribes believe our traumatic experiences, as well our actions, affect seven generations in the future. How far back can you go? What were your ancestors' circumstances? Did they immigrate to your current country? Did they grow up during a world war? Did they grow up under oppression? Were they children of the Great Depression? Did your ancestors suffer from the brutality of slavery, the Holocaust, violence, massive corruption or starvation? Were your ancestors the oppressors? Because we are all one, the pain we inflict on others, we inflict on ourselves. No one is a winner in a system where any one of us is oppressed. Wounds of a generation impact that cohort, but also their pain gets passed down through successive generations. The cellular memory of pain, struggle, limitation, and guilt from your ancestors can act like tendrils of a creeping vine that imperceptivity encroach on your heart's desires, effectively choking off their growth.

While it's important to respect our ancestors' struggles and honor their indominable spirit, we do not need to embody their pain. Many of our ancestors endured so that we would have a better life. They sacrificed so that we would not need to struggle as they did. We are, in fact, the dream of our ancestors. We are enjoying the physical freedoms our ancestors could only dream of. Let us also consciously choose the internal freedoms for which they fought. Let us embody their dream. In fact, it is up to us to do so. If we don't, we just perpetuate the generational wounds and continue a lineage of pain.

The natural evolution of consciousness brings us to a place where

we can know that we are powerful creators and we can intentionally release the influence of our ancestors' fear, struggle and oppression. We are free. We always have been, but now we know it.

Jungian therapist, Dr. Judith Rich, explains, "If we break the
chain of addiction, violence or other inherited, limiting beliefs, our
children and their children and those who follow them are given
access to possibilities not available to the ancestor. And thus, the
entire lineage evolves."

When we become consciously aware of the generational influence of our ancestors, we can choose which of those tendencies and
beliefs we want to continue in our own lives and pass down to our
children, and which ones are best left behind. We can do that with
the following exercise.

LESSON SIX, EXERCISE THREE:
RELEASING GENERATIONAL INFLUENCE

Using the columns below, write the name of your parent or ancestor, and list what struggles he or she endured. Also list the influence of the environment in which he or she grew up. In the next column list what positive qualities they possessed that you would like to embody as your own and pass down to successive generations. This is their gift to you.

Name of Ancestor	Their Struggle	Their Gift

HEALING PRAYER:

After you've identified your ancestors struggle, take a moment and hold them in your heart. All beings do the best they can with the understanding they have at the time. Your parents and grandparents inherited the wounds from *their* ancestors' generation, just as you did. It's now time to heal the whole lineage for yourself, your children, and your children's children.

Once you've connected with him or her in your heart, take out a piece of paper and write a letter to your ancestor, blessing them and declaring your freedom . . . the freedom they dreamt for you. Below is a template. Feel free to change it and write what comes from your heart.

> Dear _____: I honor you for enduring _____.
> I honor your courage and admire your tenacity. I know your dream for me was one of freedom, happiness and prosperity. I am, in fact, the embodiment of all your hopes and dreams. I claim that dream now. I release any residual pain or struggle, as well as any beliefs based in separation. I lovingly choose the freedom and happiness you dreamt for me.

EXAMPLE:

Name of Ancestor	Their Struggle	Their Gift
My mother	Grew up in The Great Depression, in a family repressed and afraid of life.	Loved people. Loved family. Had deep spiritual under-standing.
My father	Became a young man during World War II. Fought in the war.	Had really great dis-cipline and a terrific sense of humor.

Healing Prayer for Mother:

> Dear Mom: I honor you and your parents for enduring the Great Depression. I honor your courage and admire your tenacity. I know your dream and my grandparents' dream for me is one of freedom, happiness, and prosperity, and I consciously release any residual pain and sense of struggle. I consciously release the generational beliefs in lack and limitation. I consciously release

the fear you, your parents, and their parents were held captive by. I lovingly choose the freedom you dreamt for me. I choose to embody your love of people as well as your deep spiritual understanding.

Healing Prayer for Father:

Dear Dad: I honor your strength, tenacity and courage you developed in the face of a world war. I know your dream for your children was one where we would live in peace and prosperity. I consciously release any xenophobia, as well as any residual pain and psychological wounds from fighting in the war. I lovingly choose the peace and freedom you dreamt for me. I enthusiastically embrace your intelligence and your sense of humor.

INFLUENCE GOES BOTH WAYS

Because we are all connected with each other on the subjective side of life, we have many perceptions we share as a culture. Unlike the collective *un*conscious, these are, for the most part conscious. These perceptions are the prevalent beliefs our society accepts as true, generally without question. Many of these shared perceptions form the basis of our *human* awareness. If we do not make the effort to question whether or not a perception is actually true, it will likely become part of our belief system and, consequently, our experience.

Consider the common beliefs we share as a culture:

- Most marriages end in divorce.
- Most small businesses fail.
- There's no way to reverse climate change. We're pretty much doomed.
- Entrenched politicians will never pass any meaningful legislation.
- Big Business doesn't care about the little guy.
- After age 40, the physical body begins to fall apart.
- When your kids grow into teenagers, they become impossible.
- War and poverty will always be with us.

The list of shared perceptions is endless. What would you add to this list? What did you grow up believing? These beliefs become part of the fabric of our culture, and they keep us imprisoned in a cell of victimhood. They are not necessarily true, and more importantly do not need to be true for you. It is up to you to question these, and other accepted beliefs, and set up an alert system to catch them. Then ask, "Is this really true for everyone? Does it need to be true for me?" Our beliefs are powerful. Investigate them before you accept them as your own.

The good news for humanity is that as we work to shift our own beliefs and change our energy, the substance of the collective unconscious shifts as a whole. In other words, our efforts to up-level our consciousness contributes to the healing of the world. We can intentionally help create the shift. The transformation of the collective unconsciousness is up to those of us who are conscious, and we each have a unique role to play. We can consciously add into this collective mind our love, our prayers, our generous acts, our compassion and our recognition of the abundant world in which we live. All of that helps lift the heavy, oppressive, lower vibration. Then, we see that energy reflected in the world as moments of grace, healing, and unexpected good. Not only will you be empowering yourself, but you'll also be contributing to the healing of the collective unconscious, which over time, will help lift humanity out of the destructive patterns woven throughout our culture.

THE EVOLUTIONARY SHIFT

Now, many shared beliefs in the collective consciousness do shift naturally as we continue to evolve as a species. History proves this time and again. For example:

- There was a time we believed it was impossible for a human being to run a mile in less than four minutes. It was universally acknowledged that the human body was physically incapable of the challenge. Then, Roger Bannister came along and in 1954 ran it in 3:59. Suddenly the limitation was removed. Since then, runners have been steadily breaking Bannister's record.

- Twenty years ago, medical professionals insisted it was rare for women over age 40 to give birth to their first child. It was widely believed that a woman's childbearing years were in her twenties. However, since the rise of the women's movement, many women have chosen to delay parenthood to have a career. As a result, the needs of women have created an expanded consciousness. We refuse to accept the "fact" that a woman having a baby at an older age is impossible. In response to the change in consciousness, technology has risen to the occasion. Consequently, in the last decade, births to women over 39 have increased by more than fifty percent. Fertility medicine is one of the fastest growing fields in medical science. Today, it's not only possible to have a baby after 40; it's a common occurrence.[3]

- In 2008, an African American junior senator who had served in the U.S. Senate for just two years, with the impossible name of Barack Hussein Obama, was elected President of the United States, less than 150 years after the passage of the 13th amendment.

- Until recently it was illegal to marry someone of the same sex. In fact, most of the country sat in judgment and disapproval of same sex relationships. Until the '70s you really couldn't even talk about it. Since then, there has been a growing movement within our country, and within the world, initiated by young people, who saw no difference between a same sex couple marrying versus a straight couple doing the same. "Love is love," they affirmed. The idea caught fire in our collective psyche, and in 2015 the United States Supreme Court passed the Marriage Equality Act allowing all individuals to marry the one they love, regardless of gender. In 2019 and early 2020, an openly gay man had a formidable run for President of the United States.

In each of the above examples, the idea began to grow in the collective consciousness as the individual or group involved refused to accept the current limitation of the status quo, and was committed to breaking through the envelope. At some point, a critical mass was reached and the entire culture then shifted from "impossibility thinking" to "possibility thinking." As a result, freedom was *experienced* rather than limitation and powerlessness.

Roger Bannister wrote the following about his experience:

> No longer conscious of my movement, I discovered a new unity with nature. I had found a new source of power and beauty, a source I never dreamt existed.

Herein lies the key. When we connect with Source Energy, it will expose limiting core beliefs for what they are . . . self-imposed. When *our* purpose is further connected with the idea of serving a *higher* purpose we become unstoppable!

That is exactly what we are going to explore in the next chapters.

7

THE TRANSFORMATIONAL
DIMENSION

*It is rather a matter of an awakening, an awareness far be-
yond the reach of the intellect, an experience which springs
up and erupts in the deepest recesses of the soul.*

—*Abhishiktananda*

Do you remember The Beach Boys song from the '60s, "Good Vibrations"? That song was truly innovative for its time. No one, with the exception of the Beatles, was creating this kind of complex multidimensional sound. With this song, The Beach Boys also popularized the concept of "vibes." It spoke to the expanding consciousness that was occurring during the '60s. There was a dawning awareness, probably due to the influx of Indian gurus and yogis who were starting to teach in this country about the higher dimensions of our being. Those who were listening began to understand that there was indeed a vibratory field that we can't see, but that we can certainly experience, and it has an effect on every area of our lives.

It's that higher vibratory field of love that Brian Wilson sang about. It's a feel-good vibe that we instinctively want to access and play in as long as possible. But what exactly is this vibrational-field-of-love? And how can we access it intentionally?

To answer that, we need to explore the energetic nature of this universe.

Everything in the universe is indeed energy. All life is made up of atoms and all atoms are made up of subatomic particles, which of themselves are vibrations. Those particles are vibrating at different rates, depending on what form they take. The physical dimension vibrates at the fastest rate; the mental/emotional dimension vibrates at a slightly slower rate; particles in the subtle, energetic realm vibrate a little slower still, and the higher vibratory realm of love is vibrating at the slowest rate. We discussed in Chapter Three how each of us exists on all levels simultaneously—that we are, in truth, multidimensional beings that exist on a vibrational spectrum ranging from the purest level down to the densest level.

126

Now that you have worked to clear the energy that had been stuck in the lower vibrational realms using the techniques detailed in the last six chapters, you can intentionally access the highest vibratory realm and experience the numerous benefits of doing so. If you tried to go directly to the higher vibratory realms without first healing the energy in the human dimension, you would be performing a sort of "spiritual bypass." It might feel wonderful, and you may experience tremendous peace at the moment, but it's not sustainable. Before long, those unaddressed issues you have struggled with will begin to reappear in often awkward and uncomfortable ways.

This higher realm is the vibrational-field-of-love and it is a creative, fertile dimension of timelessness and pure potentiality that is responsive to our creative thought. It is a state of egolessness that allows us to connect with our highest Spiritual Self. And, yes, we can learn to *intentionally* access it. When we open to this realm, and learn to work within it, we have at our disposal a creative field of infinite possibilities.

You have, no doubt, had a taste of this subtle vibrational realm and maybe hadn't realized it. If you've ever been awestruck by a majestic view of the natural world and allowed yourself to be drawn into the wonder of it; if you've ever been transported by a wave of inexplicable joy; if you've ever been so in love with someone that you see only their true spiritual self; if you've ever been so engaged in doing something you love that time seemed to stand still; if you've ever reached a blissful transcendent state in meditation far beyond the reach of the ego, you have pierced through the thickness of the physical dimension and began to the touch this subtle, yet powerful realm.

Then there are those who have experienced total absorption into this vibrational-field-of-love. The encounter is difficult to describe, but mystics and poets have done their best to share their experience with us. Ralph Waldo Emerson explained his experience this way:

> Standing on the bare ground, my head bathed by the blithe air, and uplifted into infinite space—all mean egotism vanishes. I become a transparent eyeball. I am nothing. I see

all. The currents of the Universal Being circulate through me. I am part or particle of God.[1]

In this state the ego vanishes, the body vanishes, and any sense of separation vanishes as you dissolve into Universal Being. This is an awareness of complete oneness. It is the place where you realize you *are* the light . . . you *are* the One expressing.

In the Gospel of John, the writer's interpretation of the life and mission of Jesus is filled with "I am" statements. For example, "I am the vine and ye are the branches." "I am the light of the world." "Jesus saith unto him, I am the way, the truth, and the life: no man cometh unto the Father, but by me." This has unfortunately been misinterpreted as if Jesus was speaking from the level of his personal identity and that He, as an individual, was the "one and only." A deeper understanding reveals that He was not referring to Himself on an individual level. Rather, He was referring to the Highest level of Divine consciousness that was expressing as Him . . . *and is expressing as us all.* So, when we read, "No man cometh unto the Father but by me" it takes on a whole new meaning. We can see He was telling us that in order to embody spiritual awareness, we must "come into" that vibrational "Father" dimension of the Absolute through Christ Consciousness, or Oneness Consciousness. Once there, we can see that we are Divine Life expressing.

An interesting exploration of the multidimensionality of our being (which, incidentally, is another way to look at the Trinity) is an insight shared by a student of Ramana Maharshi, the yogi, Abhishiktananda. He compares the Christian notion of the Trinity and how it relates to the Vedic wisdom experience of non-duality. In his book entitled, *Saccidananda: A Christian Approach to Advaitic Experience*, he says,

> It is rather a matter of an awakening, an awareness far beyond the reach of intellect, an experience which springs up and erupts in the deepest recesses of the soul. The experience of Saccidananda carries the soul beyond all merely intellectual knowledge to her very center, to the Source of her being. Only there is she able to hear the Word, which reveals the undivided unity . . . the mystery of the Three

Divine Persons: in "Sat" the Father, the absolute Beginning and Source of Being; in "Cit" the Son, the Divine Word, the Father's Self-knowledge; in "Ananda" the Spirit of Love, Fullness and Bliss without end.[2]

Traditionally we understand the Trinity as being Father, Son, and Holy Spirit. In New Thought we view the Trinity as Absolute Pure Being, Individualized Expression, and the Creative, Vibrational Realm that connects the two.

It is that Creative, Vibrational Realm—or the "Ananda" realm—that is the vibrational-field-of-love we want to enter. It is in this realm that true transformation happens.

The Fillmores talked about entering this creative realm as the only effective place from which to do our Affirmative Prayer work.

Myrtle wrote this:

When we pray together in omnipresence, we lose sight of everything but the one Presence; we recognize only the spiritual Source of all things. Be still. Be still. Be still. God in the midst of you is substance. God in the midst of you is wisdom, God in the midst of you is love . . . Love is so sure and unfailing, love so irresistible and magnetic that it draws your supply to you from the great storehouse of the universe.[3]

She makes it clear that the *quality* of this vibrational realm is LOVE. It is a realm beyond all temporary forms and conditions, beyond the experience of duality, health and sickness, right and wrong, prosperity and poverty, abundance and lack. This vibrational-field-of-love is beyond all of that. And, as Myrtle suggested, we can access it by being still and knowing that "God in the midst of you is Love." We access it through the heart center, which is a porthole to that boundless ocean of Infinite Love within us. Myrtle suggests, "being still" as a very effective way to access this vibrational-field-of-love. Those who practice deep meditation on a regular basis are familiar with this state. However, it's not the only way. Some access this vibrational-field-of-love through ecstatic dance; Sufis access it through the practice of Zikr (long repetitions of mantras usually spoken together in a group with repetitive movement). Some access it through Tantric Yoga, or Kriya Yogic breathing. Others access this realm by hiking for hours in the mountains. Surfers access it by becoming one with the wave. Others access it by being in deep loving connection with their partner, or by petting their cat or dog for an extended period of time. Some access this realm by losing themselves in beautiful music, or by practicing proactive gratitude. There are many ways to enter this realm of "love-good vibrations" and we all instinctively know how to get there. The point is to do it *and* to be intentional about it. Being immersed in the vibrational-field-of-love lifts us high above the temporary, relative realm of dualistic experience, so we can know at our core the absolute truth of who we are.

One reason to intentionally access this realm is simply to experience the bliss of pure Beingness. We can also access this vibrational-field-of-love for the purpose of reimagining our lives and for drawing forth the Infinite possibilities that are within us.

MAKING IT PRACTICAL

As we discussed in Chapter Two, New Thought pioneers continually searched for a method of making this expansive way of experiencing consciousness practical. They would ask: "How do we bring this awareness into our lives so that we can experience more harmony in our relationships, more health in our bodies, more prosperity in our lives, and more peace in our world? How can we use it to help create a world that works for everyone?"

They developed a systematic approach for bringing that realm of pure potentiality into everyday experience. They realized that this vibrational-field-of-love is a realm of energy that is waiting for a specific, dynamic idea to bring unformed substance into expression as specific form and experience. In other words, when we are immersed in this realm, the creative power of our word activates potential energy, which then works to draw experiences that reflect that idea.

But we first need to engage this vibrational-field-of-love. That's the first step. The Fillmores must have had this in mind when they developed Affirmative Prayer. The first three steps are all about immersing oneself in the field.

1. Relaxation. In this step we relax not only our physical body, but also our thinking mind. We intentionally relax the mind chatter. We relax our focus on the past or future. We release our "to-do" list. We relax into the present moment and bring our awareness to our heart center. We also relax our attachment to the relative world of effect by remembering that all form and experience has its origin in Creative Mind.

2. Focus. Once we've released our focus on the relative world of effect, we can open to a higher realm . . . the realm of Creative Mind or the Absolute. The Absolute realm is one of universal limitless good. It is pure peace. It is pure love and pure joy. It is wholeness and infinite beauty. It is intelligence and creativity. In this step we focus our awareness on the Absolute and open to the qualities of this higher realm.

3. Meditation/Contemplation. In this step we allow ourselves to fully enter that vibrational-field-of-love at the center of our being. We contemplate the truth that we are an essential aspect of this one. We are an idea in the mind of the Divine—the Infinite's idea of Itself in expression. We feel at our core that all that the Infinite is, we are. We dive into that awareness and drink deeply of the waters of pure Being.

These steps help us connect with this realm of pure potentiality. Once there, the invisible substance of that vibrational realm can receive the impression of our focused thought which allows it to become realized in our experience. In the next chapter, we'll explore exactly how to do that with a new understanding of the last two steps of Affirmative Prayer.

LESSON SEVEN, EXERCISE ONE: GUIDED PROCESS FOR ACCESSING THE VIBRATIONAL-FIELD-OF-LOVE

One of the best ways of accessing that vibrational-field-of-love is through Proactive Gratitude. Proactive Gratitude is a state we generate within us by consciously choosing to see the blessing in as many things as possible. We are not waiting for something for which to be grateful. Instead, we continue searching until we find it. And what we discover is that blessings are all around us. We just had our eyes closed.

In this exercise, we will open our eyes wide to the myriad blessings in our lives and focus on them until we are lifted into the vibrational-field-of-love. To help us get there, we'll immerse ourselves in the song, "I Am So Blessed," by Karen Drucker.

When you're ready, go to my website Breakthrough2.com/exercises and click on Lesson 7, Exercise 1 to access the guided process. Alternatively, you can download Karen Drucker's song and listen while you follow the instructions.

If it feels right to you, sing along. Or, just listen and allow the music to wash over you. As it does, feel yourself bathing in the energy of gratitude while you contemplate all the areas of your life. Think about everything that is going right in each area. Consider your body: What is working well? What area of your body is feeling good and healthy? Examine your relationships. Think about all the people who love you and care about you. Think about all the people *you* love. Open your heart to all the love you receive from others and all the love you give to others. If you have a beloved pet, bring him or her to mind. Feel right now the love your pet shares with you. Now, think about your work in the world. Think about how your gifts and talents are being shared. Bring to mind anybody in your workplace you truly enjoy. If you do volunteer work, think about how it gives your life meaning to be of service to others and how others are blessed because of what you do. Consider your relative prosperity. In comparison to much of the world, think about how prosperous you are. If you have a roof over your head, a bed to sleep in at night, food to eat, money to buy a thing or two that adds joy to your life and to share with others, then you are richer than 90 percent of the world's population. Contemplate your enjoyment in life. What do you do for fun? What brings you joy? Now, consider this amazing planet. Bring to mind the vastness of the oceans, the majesty of the mountains, the endless variety of plant and animal life, etc. Then think about your spiritual growth. How have you grown spiritually in the last few years? What feeds your soul? Allow yourself to be grateful for it all.

As you contemplate all the areas that are working well and everything that is going right in your life, allow that feeling of gratitude to well up in you. Let it vibrate within your entire being. Feel it carry you into that vibrational-field-of-love.

When the song is over, silently affirm to yourself: "I am Infinite Love expressing. I am Infinite Love expressing. I am Infinite Love expressing." Affirm it over and over. Enjoy resting in that energy field of love in the silence for several minutes.

When you feel ready, take a deep, cleansing breath, and begin to bring your awareness back. Affirm that your energy field is closed to only positive energy.

Know that you can always return here. Learn what your access point is. Get familiar with the activity that brings you into the vibrational-field-of-love. It's different for everyone. Once you find what works best for you, *practice* it. All good things come to those who practice.

Next, we'll explore this transformational dimension and learn to use it to welcome our good.

8

PLAYING IN THE ENERGY OF THE ANSWER

*Play is the only way the highest intelligence
of humankind can unfold.*

—Joseph Chilton Pearce

Throughout this book, you have been gradually training to see yourself as a Spiritual Being in process of revealing more of who you truly are. You've worked to release everything that's been blocking the full expression of your Highest Self. You've had experience accessing the vibrational-field-of-love. You're beginning to grasp the concept that you are completely one with the Infinite and that everyone is an individualized point of Infinite Life, here to express the magnificence within them. As you embody this awareness, you begin to experience the Truth that you already *are* the good you seek. There is no separation. There's no place where the fullness of Spirit ends and you begin. It's not outside of you. You are the "I AM." You are the Whole expressing. As you embrace this fully, you no longer find yourself questioning your worthiness because you know that you *are it* already. It's no longer an issue of being worthy of receiving or not. You're not receiving. You *are* the Infinite Good expressing. From this awareness an abundant and joyous life naturally unfolds.

In addition, the universe is set up to support our joy and fulfillment. Life is here to support our growth, our well-being, and the realization of our highest potential. I liken it to the blossoming of a flower. Flowers are coded to bloom in the right season. That blossoming is supported naturally by fertile soil, sunshine, and rain. Having the support of Mother Nature, they will most certainly bloom. An acorn is life energy that is coded to emerge as an oak tree. It is encouraged by fertile soil to relax and release the splendor that resides within it. The sun, rain, and soil then support the emergence of an acorn's full potential.

In a similar way we are also completely supported—perhaps more so. Jesus explained in Matthew (6:27): "Consider the lilies of the field, how they grow. They toil not, neither do they spin. And yet I say to you, that Solomon in all his glory was not arrayed as one of these."

This is not just a message for Christians. This is universal wisdom that mystics and sages throughout time have understood. It's also reflected in the Tao Te Ching:

> The soft overcomes the hard; the flexible conquers the stiff; the ethereal penetrates the solid. This is why there is great advantage in stillness and silence over movement and speaking. (saying 43)

It must have been this idea that inspired Ernest Holmes who wrote in *The Science of Mind*, "To him who can perfectly practice in action, all things are possible."

And yet that goes against everything we've ever learned. What we've been taught here in the Western world is that we need to work hard to achieve. We must go out and "grab the bull by the horns." But if you think about that image, the bull would not be too happy about it and might just toss you into the air like a wet noodle.

Struggle is in our everyday language. We fight against cancer. We declare a war against drugs. We battle heart disease. We struggle and compete to get ahead. We've all been operating under a false assumption that life is a struggle. The pervasive perception in the collective unconscious is that we need to fight to get ahead, work really hard, beat the odds, make sure we win and others lose, and make it happen, even force it to happen. When we struggle to grab hold of our good believing it is "out there somewhere," we just push it further away from us.

Instead of building momentum, that forceful energy is working *against* the natural process of unfoldment. We're fighting against the universe. It's exhausting. It will wear us out and make us old before our time.

The truth is it's not your job to struggle to make things happen, or to work hard to be happy, or to figure out how to make your good manifest, or to pray diligently for months on end to convince a reluctant universe to fulfill your request. No. As you've learned so far in this book, all the good you could possibly desire is already yours. It's just a matter of first clearing out the weeds that would choke off the growth of your good and then bringing yourself into alignment with it. It's about accessing that vibrational-field-of-love and connecting with Infinite potential, then dwelling in that energy. Once there, you simply embrace the good that is present and call it forth from the Invisible.

In fact, rather than trying hard to make something happen, it's really just a matter of making your good welcome. Your only "goal" is to make the abundance, peace, joy, health, well-being, and the realization of your full Divine potential *welcome*. That's how we prepare the soil for the blossoming of our good.

To make something welcome is to prepare. Think about how you might prepare to welcome a treasured guest in your home. You would clean and straighten up your house. Maybe you'd prepare a meal, or at least put water on for tea or chill some wine. You would make your space comfortable and inviting for your guest.

In this same way, we welcome our good. We prepare our "home" by preparing our consciousness. We weed old ideas based in separation, and we release the unhealed energy that has been blocking us through the techniques previously described in this book. Then we do what we know to connect with that vibrational-field-of-love and open to the flow of good. That's really our only "work."

To continue with that same passage from Matthew, "Seek ye first the Kingdom of God, and His righteousness, (in New Thought we interpret that as "right-use-ness"—the right use of Spiritual Laws) and all else shall be added." In other words, seek to connect with the Power and Presence within and understand how it works. Seek to dwell in that vibrational-field-of-love and let it inform your thinking. From that higher awareness, you understand that your highest good is already established in the Invisible—in the Spiritual Realm. You only need to feel your way into it. In other words, it's not enough to *know* your well-being . . . or to *know* your highest and best is already established . . . you must *feel* into it. You then allow yourself to connect with the joy of its reality.

So then, what is there to pray for? Nothing. Why would you pray for something you already have? It's really more a process of affirming and embracing your good *from* a consciousness of having. More than *praying*, it's about *playing* in the energy of the answer. And that brings us back to Affirmative Prayer, which is—at its core—not prayer at all.

Let's look again at the first three steps of Affirmative Prayer:

1. **Relaxation.** In this step you want to relax not only your physical body, but also your thinking mind. Relax the mind chatter. Release the past. Let go of the future. Relax into the present moment and bring your awareness to your heart center. More importantly, you want to relax your attachment to the physical dimension. Remember that all form and experience in the relative, temporary, and changeable world of effect has its origin in Creative Mind.

2. **Focus.** Once you've released your focus on the relative world of effect, you can open to a higher realm, the realm of Creative Mind or the Absolute. The Absolute realm is one of universal limitless good. It is pure peace. It is pure love and pure joy. It is wholeness and infinite beauty. It is intelligence and creativity. In this step you focus your awareness on the Absolute and on the qualities of this higher realm.

3. **Meditation/Contemplation.** Now, allow yourself to enter that vibrational-field-of-love at the center of your being. Open to the truth that you are an essential part of this wholeness. Feel the reality of that. This is who you *are*. You are an idea in the mind of the Divine—the Infinite's idea of Itself in expression. Feel at your core that all that the Infinite is you are. From this awareness, you may want to say something to the effect of, "I live, move and have my being in limitless abundance. I am limitless abundance expressing." Or, "I live, move and have my being in wholeness and well-being. I am wholeness and well-being expressing." Dive into that awareness and drink deeply of the waters of your Divine Beingness. Feel the joy that rises in you as you do this. Let that joy radiate throughout your entire being.

These are specific steps designed to transport you into the realm of the Absolute. You want to move through them slowly, allow yourself to *feel into them*. It's not about the words; it's where the words take you—directly into that vibrational-field-of-love. That's your goal with these three steps.

Now, once you are in that vibrational field, it's time to claim your inherent good. Remember you are one with Creative Mind—that is *your* mind—so what you are doing is giving unformed substance a specific form to flow into. These next two steps will accomplish that.

1. **Realization.** In this step you allow the realization to bubble up in your awareness that anything you could ever possibly desire already exists in Divine Mind. It is already an idea, right now. That feeling you call desire is really the universe knocking on the door of your consciousness saying, *Hey, here you go. This is already yours. I've been holding it for you in escrow. Please accept it.* That's what the feeling of desire is. You would not desire it if it weren't already in existence as an idea. The universe wants to be more fully expressed through and as you. Your full potential wants to emerge and fully blossom. And you are now making it fully welcome.

Now, in order to align all levels of your being with the good that is waiting for you to accept, you will activate your power of Imagination. You are by nature a creative being and this is where you get to visualize the details of your heart's desire. Perhaps visualize is not the right word. It's more that you want to *feel* what you will feel when your good manifests. How will you feel when you are experiencing what you truly desire?

Experience it like it was in your life right now. Imagine yourself there now. Breathe it in. *Feel* your way into it. Make it rich with color, sound, depth, and texture. How does it feel to be the person you've always wanted to be? How do you feel when you express your full Divine potential? Breathe into that "reality."

2. **Gratitude and Release.** In this step you allow gratitude to well up. To be clear, you are not expressing gratitude that God has finally heard your prayer, or that you have faith your good will manifest. You are grateful for the *reawakening* in your consciousness of

who you truly are now. It is understanding that sets us free. You are grateful for the awareness that the good you are affirming for yourself already exists in the invisible realm and it is now in process of blossoming in your experience. It's happening. Your heart's desire is a bud that is now opening and revealing the fragrance that has been there in potential.

Secondly, you want to release this whole Affirmative Prayer process to the universe, and in doing so, release concern about the "how." Instead of being concerned with *how* your heart's desire is going to unfold, or being attached to a specific outcome, you want to be receptive to the instruction of your Inner Wisdom . . . *then follow its guidance.*

At the end of your Affirmative Prayer session you should feel empowered, joyous, fearless, even exalted. You should feel the fullness of your Authentic Self. It should feel more like a joyous dance of glorious energy. It should feel like *play.* In fact, what you are doing is not praying. You are playing! You are playing in the energy of the answer. This is the secret. This is what brings forth your good. It should be a joyous process of preparing the soil by immersing yourself in pure Beingness and creating the conditions that *allow* the good that is already yours to blossom.

And this is what it means to practice inaction. It's not really complete inaction, because as you can see, there's a lot of shifting taking place in consciousness. But it can appear as inaction to the world.

That doesn't mean you don't move your feet. But you move your feet *only* following Divine Guidance. You move your feet with joy. You dance into your wholeness. This is how you make your good welcome. Now, that doesn't mean it won't be uncomfortable. In fact, there is always some discomfort involved in growth, in expanding our sense of self. We'll talk more about that in the next chapter.

WORKING WITH THE SUPPORT OF THE UNIVERSE

About three years ago I had a vision of living next to a lake. There is something about the stillness of water that's so healing. It just feeds my soul. It stills my mind and fills me with peace. The ocean can do that too, but even more so with a lake. A friend of mine pointed out, "Of course, Victoria, you're a water sign—that make sense." I guess so.

So, I set my intention to find a house on a lake. My husband, Dana, and I were starting to talk at the time about downsizing since our children were about to go off to college. There was no longer a reason to have five bedrooms and five bathrooms. Also, as beautiful as our house was, it was sort of dark inside. We both wanted more light. I shared my vision with him, and it turned out he liked the idea too. So, I got to work on preparing my consciousness. The first thing I did was begin the Affirmative Prayer process. I dove into the feeling nature of it—imagining what it would be like sitting having coffee out on the deck, watching the sun rise over the lake, or chillin' with my hubby in the evening watching the sun set and ducks landing on the water. Maybe there'd be a great blue heron (in animal medicine the blue heron represents self-worth). Next, I created a vision board. I searched the internet and found some pictures taken from inside a house situated beside a lake, looking out onto the water. I placed them on my vision board, and began some visualization around this.

Then we began looking. We told our real estate agent to start looking. We all looked, and looked and looked. Before long we discovered that, in our area, there wasn't much choice. We went to look at a property on a lake that was 45 minutes out of town. It was a beautiful lake, but just too far, and too rural for us. We hoped that maybe we'd find something on the lake that happened to be right in the center of our town. But houses on that lake start around $1.5 million . . . *for a fixer-upper*. So that was out. We saw some houses with small ponds in back. Those weren't right either. After a year of searching, we eventually gave up the dream of being on the water. We started looking at regular, inland houses. For two years we looked at all kinds of houses. Some I really liked, but Dana hated. Or Dana liked, but I hated. We just couldn't agree. Fortunately, we had a very patient real estate agent. For a time we considered building our own house. We searched and searched for the right lot, but we couldn't find it.

Admittedly, most of this effort to find a new home was coming from me. My husband was in no hurry to move. I basically had to drag him. It all started getting a little crazy. I noticed I was becoming obsessed. Once I finally admitted that, I had to do some work releasing my attachment and making peace with where we were. I had to let go.

Well, a funny thing happened. Once I did that, Dana started stepping up his effort to look. He was suddenly motivated to find the right house. He'd look at the listings every day and say, "What do you think about this? What about that?" But again, nothing was right.

Then, one day, I went back to my vision board and looked again at those images of the house looking out onto a lake. A voice inside said, *This is your original vision . . . stay with it.* The human part of me said, "Well, I *did* and there was nothing. It's not possible." But my Inner Wisdom kept insisting, *It's all possible, keep preparing your consciousness. Make your good welcome.*

About two months later, we found it. Dana found it. A house right on a lake! It was a house with lots of windows through which we could look out onto the lake. It was also in town, in a neighborhood with which I was completely unfamiliar. Our real estate agent knew the neighborhood, but had no idea there was a lake. The house was the right size for the two of us, plus our kids when they came home to visit. Also it was very bright with floor-to-ceiling windows. Everything was perfect with the exception of one thing: It was way over our budget. The house was truly overpriced. We decided to look at it anyway. The moment we walked in the door, we both fell in love. We *both* loved it. Now, the only thing to do was wait. We had to wait for the seller to realize they'd overpriced it and bring down the asking price. Weeks went by.

During that time, we had a grand opportunity to practice inaction. As I mentioned, while it looks like inaction to the outside world, there's usually lots of growth occurring in consciousness! In that downtime, I added photos from the actual house to my vision board. I spent time immersing myself in the vibrational-field-of-love and did my visualization. While engaged in Affirmative Prayer, I visualized myself being in that house. I saw myself walking around the house, being in the bedroom with big windows that looked right onto the lake. I saw myself having coffee in the screened-in porch overlooking the lake. Mentally, I was already living in that house.

At the same time, I was working on not being too attached. I wanted to truly feel okay if this particular house didn't work out. It's a delicate balance between passionately embracing your vision and not getting attached to it. It's a balance I'd never mastered before, so this was a chance to grow into it.

About a month passed. Then on Friday night, as we were driving in the rain to have dinner with friends, our agent called to let us know the sellers received another offer on the house, and if we wanted it, we'd have to make an offer now. Our offer had to be higher than originally intended. We took some deep breaths, listened to our inner guidance, and went ahead and made an offer, well below what the sellers were asking.

That was when I had to activate trust. I had to totally trust and let go. This was the biggest stretch for me. The odds were against us. Why would they take a lesser offer? I ramped up my Affirmative Prayer and visioning work to continue creating the conditions in consciousness for my good to grow. A lot happened that weekend—much back and forth—a lot of working numbers. Then it happened. We got the call that they accepted our offer, and we went under contract the following Tuesday.

Now we had to sell *our* house. We thought that would be a piece of cake. It was a beautiful home in a desirable neighborhood, and we had been preparing it for sale. It "showed very well." We had a buyer that first weekend and went under contract. Then, during their inspection, they discovered a problem—a big problem. There was something fundamentally wrong with the plumbing throughout the house, an issue we'd never been aware of. But there it was. We lost our buyer, and it looked like we were facing tens of thousands in repair bills and a month or more off the market. With that hit we could not make the down payment on the new house.

Here we were in limbo, all hopes dashed. We were going to lose our dreamhouse. I think I spent a couple days releasing a bucket of tears over it. But, at the same time, that inner voice kept telling me that somehow it would all work out. Remember, I was already *living* in the new house mentally and vibrationally. Even though I could not see *how* it was going to work, I knew something was going to shift that would allow it to happen.

I decided it was time to get to work visualizing a wonderful new family living in our current house, loving it the way we did, with children playing in the fenced-in back yard, as ours had done. I imagined the parents walking their kids to school down the forested path behind the house that I used to walk my kids to school.

One day, in casual conversation with a neighbor, this man mentioned that he'd had a similar plumbing problem with a previous home. He told me about a solution he discovered that was a fraction of the amount we were facing and could be done in a day or so. "What? Really? And this worked?" "Yes," he assured me. My husband did some further research on this system and discovered that it would indeed do the trick. We had the work done and got the house back on the market in less than a week.

After our second open house, our agent called with three offers. She said one of them had written a letter to us, and she asked if she could she read it to us. "Absolutely, please do." The letter was written by the mother of two children who absolutely fell in love with our home. She wrote that they'd been looking for more than a year for that "right house" but hadn't found it until they walked into ours. She wrote that they loved what we'd done with it, and could see her children playing in the back yard. The family felt like it was their home. Also, by the way, theirs was the higher offer. "Yes, we're selling our house to them. Call them now and tell them *yes*."

Not only did we sell our house at full price and in record time, but we also sold it to a family we knew would love living there. Just like the people who sold us the lake house, we wanted a family to live in our old home who would love it as much as we did.

Against almost impossible odds, a little more than two years from the time I had the vision, we now live in that house. I'm writing this chapter while sitting in the screened-in porch overlooking the lake. And, just now, a great blue heron flew by. I could never have made that happen. The way the universe supports our efforts when we make our good welcome is truly miraculous!

WHAT'S YOUR DREAM?

What makes *your* heart sing? What feeds your soul? Deep down you know what it is. You just have to listen to your heart. When you discover it, embrace it. Create the conditions in your consciousness for that good to blossom. Make it welcome by opening to that vibrational-field-of-love through the Affirmative Prayer process. Create a vision board with images that represent that desire, and visualize yourself having it—living it—being it. Feel your way into it. Keep your heart open. Affirm that the realization of your good is a blessing to everyone. This is how you make your good welcome.

Affirm this over and over: "I am making my good welcome."

And, finally, let go of the how. The how is not your job. Let go of the struggle. Keep listening to your inner guidance *and follow it.* Take action *only* following inner guidance and feel the joy in that action. The realization of your highest good is a natural process when you make it welcome.

LESSON EIGHT: EXERCISE ONE:
WRITE YOUR AFFIRMATIVE PRAYER

Review the content under each of the steps of Affirmative Prayer listed on the previous pages. Sit with it for a while, and let yourself begin to feel what the words mean. Then, in your own words, write your own Affirmative Prayer for your heart's desire, in the spaces below.

1. Relaxation

_____

_____

_____

_____

_____

2. Focus

_____

_____

_____

_____

_____

3. Meditation/Contemplation

_____

_____

_____

_____

_____

_____

4. Realization

_____

_____

_____

_____

_____

_____

5. Gratitude and Release

_____

_____

_____

_____

_____

_____

When you've completed writing the words of your Affirmative Prayer, take a few minutes to sit in a favorite meditation spot and read them back to yourself. As you do, let yourself feel the meaning of the words. Let it take you into that vibrational-field-of-love and enjoy playing in that energy. Enjoy the experience of fully realizing who you truly are and allowing that which you desire to blossom naturally.

CREATING YOUR INTENTION MANDALA

The kind of vision board I have found most effective is an Intention Mandala. It's like a vision board, but with the added dimension of sacred geometry. Your Intention Mandala will become a *physical symbol* of your vision, sort of like a "visual prayer." Like a blueprint for a building, your mandala presents a vibrant image directly to the *subconscious*. It bypasses the part of your brain that might think, "I could never have that" or, "that will never work."

In addition, the shape of the mandala adds sacred energy that empowers the realization of those images in profound ways. The word "mandala" in Sanskrit literally means "magic circle" and they are believed to encircle, or contain, in sacred energy, whatever is inside them.

The famous psychotherapist, Carl Jung believed that mandalas assist our "inborn urge to grow toward wholeness . . . and into the full expression of our potential."

LESSON EIGHT, EXERCISE TWO: GIVE YOURSELF AN HOUR OR MORE TO COMPLETE THIS EXERCISE.

Supplies you will need:

- Glue stick
- Pencils and markers
- Scissors
- A variety of magazines, or images printed from an online Google search
- Poster board
- Extra-large round serving platter or bowl

STEP 1:

Place the round platter or serving bowl on top of the poster board and draw around the edge with a pencil, making a large circle. Next, create a center circle by drawing either free form or use a drinking glass to trace around. The idea is to have a center and six shapes radiating out from it. Each shape represents an aspect of your life and the center represents your spiritual essence. For example, you could have a flower with six petals radiating out from the center, or a six-pointed star, or six flute shapes flowing out from a round center, or six circles surrounding a larger center circle.

The reason you want to include each area of your life rather than focusing on just the area of your major concern is this: All aspects of your life work together. Nothing exists independently. For example, say you want to realize a fulfilling and successful career. First, you'll want to find images that represent for you a joyous, fulfilling, and successful career where you are expressing your unique gifts. But you don't want to sacrifice your mental or physical health in pursuit of a big career, so you'll also want to include images of health and well-being which will support you in realizing your dreams. You also don't want to sacrifice relationships. Strong, loving, encouraging relationships will support you in your effort. You'll want to include images of prosperity and financial health as well. Prosperity might be a result of the career, but not necessarily. You might truly desire a career that doesn't historically pay well. Also, you'll want to include images that represent fun and adventure. All areas of our life are nurtured when we're having fun and life just works better. Finally, include images that represent personal and spiritual growth, which is the core that nourishes everything else. When other areas of our lives are working well, they support us in the realization of our dreams—and in the enjoyment of that dream when it is realized.

STEP 2:

Decide which of the six petals, flutes, star shape, or circles will represent particular aspects of your life. The six aspects are: Health, Finances, Career or Creative Self-expression, relationships, spiritual and personal growth, and fun and adventure. At the center of your Intention Mandala is the heart of your vision. What image might represent the core from which your desire springs? What core quality would support all the other aspects of your life? Choose this image carefully.

Where do you find the images that go on your Intention Mandala? You can either look through magazines to find images that visually represent your heart's desire. Or you can type a word or two that represents your desire into a Google image search. For instance, "inner peace" or "abundant life" or "loving relationships" or "successful women entrepreneur" or "healthy and flexible" or "house on a lake." You will be amazed at all the images that come up. Scroll through and choose the ones that speak to you. Then print them out.

You may also want to type out words or phrases that represent your vision and print those out. Alternatively, most stores that carry scrapbooking supplies will have colorful stickers with words that may match the vision you wish to express. For example, I bought a sticker sheet with the words love, peace, kindness, wonder, friendship, laugh, nurture, treasure, and miracle. I've used them all!

Below is a graphic to show you what the sections might look like:

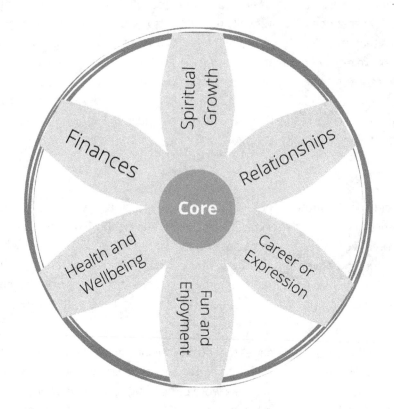

STEP 3:

Now organize all your pictures, stickers, and words on the poster board within the flower petals, stars, shapes or circles you've drawn. Arrange them in a manner that is pleasing to your eye, and then use the glue stick to attach the cutouts in place. You may also want to draw directly on the board. The process should feel like a moving meditation. You may want to play some inspiring music that feeds your creativity. Don't think about it too much, just get into the flow and enjoy!

STEP 4:

This is the most important step . . . and the one most people either don't know about, or forget. They look at their vision board or Intention Mandala and eventually think, "Well, that's not my life. It's what I wish, but it's not mine now." Instead, what you want to do is embody the understanding that it is yours now. This step will help you fully integrate the images on your mandala into your subconscious.

More than one hundred years ago, visionary author, Wallace Wattles, explained in his book, *The Science of Getting Rich*:

> Something more is necessary, however, than merely to see the picture clearly . . . behind your clear vision must be the purpose to realize it; to bring it out in tangible expression. And behind this purpose must be an invincible and unwavering faith that the thing is already yours; that it is "at hand" and you have only to take possession of it . . . be as thankful for it all the time as you expect to be when it has taken form.[1]

Wattles is really talking about *acceptance*—your ability to fully accept that you *can* have, and in fact already *do* have, the good you so desire. To achieve this level of acceptance, repeat, with as much feeling as you can muster, a positive declaration such as the one below while gazing upon your Intention Mandala:

> *This is how my Highest Self sees my life; therefore, it is already established in the invisible. I consciously align all levels of my being with my Highest Self to allow this vision to come forth in my experience now. I rejoice that this vision, or something better, is blossoming in my life now!*

And if you really want to supercharge it, strike a Power Pose while you're looking at your mandala and then say the affirmation. In other words, stand tall with your feet apart, chest uplifted, chin up, and hands on your hips like Wonder Woman. Alternatively, stand with your arms reaching the sky with your body taking the shape of a star. (For more on power poses, check out Amy Cuddy's TED talk.)

View your Intention Mandala while repeating the above positive declaration at least twice a day. Allow this process to generate feelings of joy and excitement within you. Feel that you *are* this person *now*, that this is your life *now*. Feel that this is a present-tense experience rather than a future one. Remember, your creative right brain cannot tell the difference. Before you know it, things and experiences will appear in your life, which look amazingly similar to those pictured in your mandala.

I've created Intention Mandalas (and their cousins, vision boards) a few times in my life, and when I look back on them a year or so later, I realize I've manifested many of the things exactly as pictured on the board, including the completed book, the career, the home, and even the engagement ring that looked identical to the picture I had on the board! But more importantly, I've become the person I always wanted to be.

9

PLAYING IN THE ANSWER WHEN IT'S CHALLENGING

We either make ourselves miserable, or we make ourselves
strong. The amount of work is the same.

—*Carlos Castaneda*

Okay, so you've now got some good tools to work with—tools that can assist you in allowing your highest good to fully blossom. Let's say you've totally engaged in this process. You begin your day with your Affirmative Prayer, which you understand is not a prayer at all, but a technique that allows you to play in the energy of the answer. You've created your Intention Mandala and are visualizing and embracing the feeling of now *having* your desired good. You are feeling your way into the experience of being the highest possible version of yourself. You've been dancing in that vibrational-field-of-love on a regular basis and are truly enjoying it. You are, in fact, welcoming your good, and the universe is supporting its emergence.

But let's say you're having a challenging day. The difficulties in your life are beginning to creep back into your awareness. All of a sudden you have doubts about your desired good being in process of manifesting. Maybe that pain in your back is screaming at you, causing you to feel that your body is still firmly stuck in the human realm. Or maybe you get a notice from your bank stating that your account is overdrawn and you know your paycheck is not coming for another week. Or late at night you feel an emptiness, as you have yet to find that special someone with whom you want to share your life. Or you are faced with making an important decision and can't seem to get any clear guidance. Or you just received another rejection letter on the project that is your life's dream. You sink into disappointment and are tempted to feel as though nothing has really changed. You feel as if you are back at square one.

What do you do then?

One cannot remain in that vibrational-field-of-love 24/7. It takes real effort to consistently know at your core that you are the Infinite Divine expressing when you're stuck in your "humanness" It can be challenging to consistently know that what you desire is already an idea in the mind of the Infinite and is right now in process of emerging. The human, physical dimension is dense and seductive. When you're held captive in the relative world of effect it's sometimes tempting to feel as if all the efforts you are investing in this process are useless. The experience is akin to staring at your garden bed and wondering why you're not seeing a flower blossom, even though you planted the seed only a few days ago. You're tempted to think nothing is happening and you've just wasted your time. And yet, there is so much growth happening under the surface. Keep watering and weeding—and trust—and you will see something beautiful spring forth at the right time.

There is, in fact, a bit of a time delay for that spiritual idea you have embraced to work through the dense time-bound physical dimension and blossom into experience. Ernest Holmes talked about this process in *The Science of Mind*: "The Truth is instantaneous in its demonstration, taking only such time in Its unfoldment as is inherent in the law of logical and sequential evolution."

So while you're waiting for the idea you've embraced to come to fruition, your goal is to dwell in a place of trust and keep yourself centered in that higher vibration by developing a playful, creative attitude.

Playing in the energy of the answer is a way of being that must be nurtured. It's what is referred to in Scripture as "praying without ceasing." As you've learned, you're not really praying at all, but intentionally *dancing* in that vibrational-field-of-love as much as possible. And when that become difficult—as it does from time to time for everyone—you can pull out a tool from your toolbox, a tool that helps remind you of who you truly are, and brings you back into that transformational dimension. These tools are what I call Pattern Interrupters, as they help interrupt the old patterns that keep us stuck in old ways of thinking and feeling. They shift the energy from the place that was keeping us spinning in circles, and put us back on track.

In those moments when you're caught in your humanness, in your fear, in your attachment to the relative world of effect and it appears solid and untransmutable, try one of these pattern interrupters.

PATTERN INTERRUPTER #1: GRATITUDE WALK

Put down whatever you're doing, get up and go for a walk outside. If you can, walk in nature, although a city street will do in a pinch. As you're walking, pay attention to your breath and become conscious that you are sharing that breath with all of creation. The trees welcome the breath you exhale—they need the carbon dioxide to feed their cells. In return, they produce and share the oxygen you need. Open your awareness to the fact that it is one breath, one Life, shared in a synchronous way with every living thing.

As you walk, listen to the birds singing. Take in the fragrance of the flowers or evergreens that may be on your path. Look up at the sky. Express your gratitude for each of these things. Say in your mind, "Thank you, beautiful bird, for your song. Thank you, trees, for your shade, oxygen, and beauty. Thank you, flowers, for your fragrance that fills the air. Thank you, bees, for doing such a great job ensuring plants and flowers continue to grow. Thank you, stones that have been turned into the pavement that makes my walk smooth and solid. Thank you, sun, for your warmth and allowing all life to exist." You get the idea. Then as you feel that vibration of gratitude expanding within you, affirm that the very Life Force from which all creation emanates, is the same Life Force that is guiding and governing your life. Remind yourself that it is the nature of the universe to emerge from a seed idea, to grow and blossom into its full potential. That same impulse is working within you right now! By the end of your walk you should be back on track and filled with joyful energy.

PATTERN INTERRUPTER #2: DANCE AND SING

When you find your mind spinning in a downward direction of fear, disappointment or doubt, try putting on your favorite piece of upbeat music (you know, the one that would get you up on the dance floor at your friend's wedding.) Then, either get up and dance, or sing at the top of your lungs—whatever is more enlivening for you. Maybe both. Keep doing it until you feel positive energy moving through your body infusing your mind with joy, love, and the awareness that all is indeed well. You can even do this in your car. Obviously you can't get up and dance, but you can turn up the music, move your shoulders and torso, and you can certainly sing! As you're feeling that joyous energy fill your being, affirm that it is the same joyful energy now at work, shaping substance around your desire for Infinite Good and bringing it into your experience.

PATTERN INTERRUPTER #3: AN AP CALL

Nothing gets you back on track faster than connecting with someone who is already steeped in the consciousness of wholeness and Infinite Good. That someone might be a person trained in Affirmative Prayer. Here are two resources for you:

- Silent Unity has been operating continuously for almost a century now. The prayer ministry is how Unity began. Today they have trained, dedicated, heart-centered prayer chaplains on duty to answer prayer requests from all over the world, 24 hours a day, 7 days a week. Although solidly New Thought, their focus tends toward Christian. The number to call is: (816) 969-2000.
- If you respond to a more universal spirituality, you might want to call the prayer line at Agape's International Center of Truth. Agape is where I trained in Affirmative Prayer and the Prayer Ministry is where I did my internship. The prayer practitioners here are steeped in Spirit. They have a selection of beautiful

pre-recorded prayers for common requests. In addition, a Prayer Practitioner will call you back if your leave your contact number. The Agape Prayer Hotline is: (310) 348-1270.

PATTERN INTERRUPTER #4: SELF-FORGIVENESS BOOST

We all do the best we can. So do you. It takes work to be able to see beyond the limitations of the relative world and perceive the realm of Absolute Good. We all get pulled into our humanness and forget who we truly are and where we came from. Embrace yourself in love. Hug yourself right now. While in your own embrace, go back to the exercise on Self-Forgiveness and repeat the affirmation there. Tell yourself you are an extraordinary person, doing an amazing job navigating your way through the maze and allowing yourself to be pulled by the light. Most people don't even try. You don't need to get it perfect. It's not about perfection. Your dreams will be realized even if you have moments, or even days, of doubt and fear. You might find it helpful to listen to the guided Meditation on Self-Love which will support you in this effort. You can find it on my website, Breakthrough2.com/exercises.

PATTERN INTERRUPTER #5: POWER POSES WITH AFFIRMATION

In the last chapter I mentioned the effectiveness of Power Poses. These are the physical poses that intentionally increase helpful hormones in your body and decrease the stress hormone, cortisol. They have the effect of helping you own your power. They were made famous by social science researcher, Amy Cuddy. The idea is to stand tall with your feet apart, chest uplifted, chin up and hands on your hips like Wonder Woman, or with your arms reaching toward the sky like Starman. I've also found the Warrior 2 pose in yoga to be just as effective. (To see exactly how this works, go to my website, Breakthrough2.com/videos where I demonstrate each pose.)

Now, here's how to supercharge this process: Strike one of these poses and hold it for a full two minutes. While you are holding the pose breathe deeply into your heart center. From your core affirm something like: "I am a beautiful emanation of Divine Love." Or, "I am calm, confident, peaceful, poised and centered in my spiritual Truth." Or, "I am a vibrant, vital expression of Life Energy, fully alive and present in the now moment." Affirm the spiritual truth of your being that you would like to experience right now.

This is a potent Pattern Interrupter that activates your highest self and gets it into every level of your being—spirit, mind, body, subconscious and heart.

PATTERN INTERRUPTER #6: GET GUIDANCE, TAKE ACTION

If you get stuck in the feeling that nothing is moving forward for you in the direction of your dreams, follow the instructions here for connecting with your inner guidance and taking action.

Taking action will change the energy and get you back into the flow.

There is an ancient proverb that says: "Let us go now and wake up our luck."

It's a short proverb, but rich with instruction. It tells us that our "luck" (our good fortune) is already here—it only needs to be awakened. And how do we awaken it? By "going." In other words, by taking action. When is the best time to do this? "Now!" Wisdom indeed. Let us take action now, follow our inner guidance, and *receive* the realization of our heart's desires.

When you fully welcome your good, the universe naturally conspires to support you. But that doesn't mean you can just sit back and expect bags of gold to appear on your doorstep, or the partner of your dreams to suddenly knock on your door. In order to *receive* the realization in this human dimension you must take action—but not just any action. It's far more effective to take action following your inner guidance. Below are steps for developing the ability to hear your inner guidance, and follow it into action.

1. Go into the silence, either through meditation or by simply closing your eyes, breathing into your heart center and consciously connecting with your highest Divine Wisdom.

2. Once you feel connected, ask the question, "What do *I* need to do in the physical world to facilitate the realization of my dream?"

Then, simply listen. You may receive the answer right away and it may be as clear as if someone whispered in your ear. An image may come to you, or, you may get just an overall feeling. Or, perhaps when you're not focused on it, the answer you seek will come later. A similar phenomenon occurs when you forget a person's name. While you're concentrating on remembering the name, your mind is constricted. Later, after you've let it go and are focusing on something else, the name spontaneously comes to mind (sometimes in the middle of the night)! In the same way, as you focus on other activities, the direction you're looking for will often pop into your mind. It may be two days after you've made the request, and you could be sitting in your dentist's waiting room thumbing through your phone's newsfeed. Suddenly you see something that triggers the subconscious and the answer bursts out of you, "That's what I need to do, join that networking group I heard about!" Others may look at you like you're nuts but you just smile to yourself, knowing that this is indeed the guidance you had requested.

Another way to access your intuitive wisdom is to journal. You may find journaling even more helpful in hearing your inner guidance. Use the exercise below to assist you in this process.

1. Write down the question, "What actions do I need to take in the physical world to help facilitate the birth of my dream?"

2. Your answer could appear as a stream of consciousness, a seemingly unrelated explosion of ideas, an image or several images, or a well-organized "to-do" list. Maybe you write just one simple action step. It's all good. Allow your Inner Wisdom

to guide your thoughts, and your hand, in writing down those ideas in your journal or use the space provided here.

_____

_____

_____

_____

_____

_____

_____

_____

3. Once you've received the first instruction, even if it doesn't seem to make much sense at the moment, or fit into your other plans, or relate to anything you've ever done before—act upon it. Even if it begins to bring up your fear, act upon it. You must trust enough to take the first step. When you do, you will be sending your Inner Wisdom a message that you are taking this seriously. Your Inner Wisdom will continue to support your intention. Generally, only after you've followed the first instruction will you be given the next step. You then take action on this new instruction. Soon, you'll be given another, and so on. Before you know it you're walking on a clearly marked path, your fulfillment plainly in view. Be grateful for the guidance and celebrate each step of the way toward the realization of your full Divine Potential.

This is how you build a relationship with your Inner Wisdom. It will not fail you. Your inspired action will be far more productive than your own self-initiated plans. There seems to be an unspoken agreement in this culture that the busiest person wins. But we know that's really not the case. All that going, doing, and busyness does not necessarily get us anywhere. When your activity is self-initiated (i.e., ego-led) it is often confused and ineffective. However, when you allow the Divine Wisdom within you to guide your every step, you move out into the world on purpose and achieve far more in less time.

HOW IT WORKS IN REAL LIFE

Now, let's put this all together and explore how playing in the answer might work in the four main areas of life people tend to get stuck. Each of these guides assumes you have worked through the exercises detailed thus far in the book, including embracing your true magnificent self, healing and reintegrating the shadow self, having an ongoing practice of releasing toxic emotions, and forgiving yourself and others.

Love and Relationships

Let's say you truly desire to experience more love in your relationships. Or maybe you're interested in attracting a partner and being in a committed relationship. Either way, your goal is to connect with and *play* in the energy of abundant love. You've written your Affirmative Prayer and created your Intention Mandala in order to create the conditions in consciousness that makes your desired good welcome.

To fully embrace the power of love within you, it's helpful to understand the true nature of love. Love is not, as some perceive it, a wimpy emotion. And romantic love is only a small expression of the larger power of Universal Love. Rather than being emotionally tied to a specific person, love is a power within you. The power of love is literally the force that creates and maintains the entire universe. Universal Love is a powerful energy that can be generated within you. It is a "state of being" you create by choice, and can enhance by playing in its energy. One way to do this is by contemplating the love you feel for, say, your spouse, members of your family, your pet, a best friend, a beloved spiritual teacher, your home, or your garden. You could focus on the love you have for your favorite activity, a piece of music or art, a location, or the love you feel surrounded by the beauty of nature. Begin by contemplating that thing, person or experience that speaks to you and encourage this state of love to expand within your heart, then into your entire energetic field. Focus your attention on love and permit this feeling to vibrate within your being. With practice, you'll notice that the energy of love becomes untethered to any person, place or thing. The power of Universal Love does not need an object. In addition, you want to feel at your core that you are an expression of this Infinite Love. Just as a sunbeam cannot be separate from the sun because it is, in fact, the sun expressing, you are Source expressing. You are love expressing.

Another helpful tool to expand this love within you is the Meditation for Self-Love found on my website. Also, Power Poses with Affirmations is another great way to allow the energy of positive, powerful love to move through your vibrational body.

Open your heart to the power of Universal Love and allow it to spill over into your life. This love carries a healing, renewing energy, which may be utilized for yourself and others. See your life and those around you through the eyes of this love.

Try this little experiment:

Wherever you go, consciously radiate love. Imagine you are a center of love energy. With each inhale you are generating more love-energy and with each exhale you radiate that abundant love to all those around you! You can consciously radiate this Infinite Love out to others while waiting in line at the supermarket, sitting in traffic, sitting in a theater, in your office, or amidst a crowd of any kind. When you meet anyone, focus directly on the true Divine Self at their core. This is the meaning of Namaste. "The Divine in me greets the Divine in you." Treat others with kindness, love, and forgiveness, and observe what happens. Kindness, love, and forgiveness will return to you multiplied.

Now, let's say you're engaged in this practice and are feeling great. Then, one day, a friend, family member or workmate says something really nasty to you. Maybe they hate your idea and they don't hold back letting you how stupid it is. Perhaps you just found out this person has been talking smack behind your back. Maybe he or she betrayed your trust. This is obviously a moment where it's going to be a challenge radiating your love to others. Maybe their remarks or behavior really sting and you're tempted to lash back. What do you do now?

First of all, as we discussed in Chapter Three, allow yourself to feel your feelings. Don't react from that place, but allow them to be. Later, when this moment has passed and you have some time to yourself, you may want to do one of the exercises mentioned in the chapter that releases these emotions so they don't become stored in your body.

As you recalibrate, remember that all of us are on a journey of awakening and some have taken the path that's 180 degrees away from yours. On this journey most of us have unresolved shadows that tend to sabotage our good intentions. That might be what this person is experiencing. What you're witnessing is not their highest self, but their unhealed shadow self that has become triggered. With that awareness, it becomes easier to forgive them, and return to your loving center.

If that feeling of hurt, anger or disappointment lingers, try one of the Pattern Interrupters such as the Gratitude Walk, Dance and Sing, or maybe Power Poses with Affirmations. If you choose the latter, you may find it helpful to affirm: "I am a beautiful emanation of Divine Light. I am a powerful expression of Infinite Love."

If your desire is to improve your existing relationships and experience more love, follow the steps above for listening to your Inner Wisdom and take action for if, when, and how to open up a conversation with the person who hurt your feelings.

If your true desire is to find a partner with whom you can have a committed relationship, you'll want to follow your inner guidance and take action. Once again, taking action is how we receive our heart's desires. You'll want to get out into a variety of social situations as much as possible and meet new people.

Taken together, these exercises build the awareness of love's presence—which is your very essence—and amplifies the attractive energy of love within you that radiates to others. Your relationships will begin to reflect this truth. All your interactions will become more loving, healings will happen, and if it is your true desire, the right individual will appear . . . *and you will be ready for them!* You won't sabotage it.

Finances

Let's say you want to experience more prosperity in your life. Again, we're going to assume you've already written your Affirmative Prayer and created an Intention Mandala filled with vibrant images that provoke feelings of joyous abundance.

To continue to play in the energy of abundance throughout the day, consider embracing things and/or experiences that help you *feel* rich. For some, that could be having fresh cut flowers every week arranged in a beautiful vase. For others, it might be a striking piece of art hung prominently in your living room. Maybe the splurge that makes you feel abundant is a regular spa treatment. When I was a teenager, my mother (who was not wealthy, but neither was she poor) would take me to have afternoon tea in a fancy hotel. We would then relax in the lobby and take in the scenery, just breathing in the energy of prosperity in which we were temporarily included. That was a little splurge that made us both feel truly wealthy. Whatever gives you the feeling of being abundant, do it. Splurge a little. And when you're looking at the fresh flower arrangement, or enjoying your spa treatment, or in the place that exudes wealth, breathe it in. Play in that energy. Say in your mind, "I totally deserve this. I am abundant and treat myself well. I am open to receiving. I allow myself to enjoy the prosperity that is mine now."

Another technique that can help you play in the energy of prosperity is to ponder and appreciate the symbols of abundance in nature. Go outside and look at all the leaves on one tree. See if you can count them. Then multiply that by all the trees there might be in a forest. If you're at the ocean, think about how many grains of sand there are on a beach. Countless. Then look at the sea. Imagine how many gallons of water there might be in just one ocean, not to mention all the oceans on this planet. Consider taking a drive out to the desert or mountains—anywhere that's far from city lights—and gaze up at the night sky. The abundance of stars is truly breathtaking. Think about the fact that when you see one point of light, it could be an entire galaxy with billions of stars and planets. Breathe in the abundance of the universe in which you live, move, and have your being. Rejoice in the reality that the same limitless Life Force that expresses as the abundance in nature is the Life Force that expresses as you. You are equally abundant.

If you're tempted to feel poor when viewing your bank balance, remember that your bank balance is a snapshot of yesterday's consciousness. Your current experience is the result of yesterday's thinking—when you may have had difficulty accepting abundant good. Feel in your bones that your experience tomorrow will reflect the consciousness you are building today—a consciousness that embraces the infinite good that is flowing in, around, and through you. Do a Gratitude Dance. Dance in that energy of abundance that is yours now and is in process of manifesting in your experience.

Do you have difficulty feeling abundant when you see someone driving a beautiful, expensive car, living in your dream home, traveling the world with ease, generously supporting the arts, or giving abundantly to causes you hold dear? Do you find yourself just wishing you had that level of prosperity, but thinking you never will? If so, you may find that this simple technique shifts your consciousness about it: In your mind say to this person, "I celebrate your ability to allow limitless Substance to flow through you and manifest as abundant prosperity in your life. I too am learning to allow that same limitless Substance to flow through me and manifest in my life as abundant prosperity." Know that the same amount of abundant Substance that is within them is within you—right now! We all have an equal amount of Substance. It's never a matter to getting something "out there." It's always a matter of knowing and owning what's already within us.

Many people have shadows around money. It's understandable. We live in a culture that encourages us to want more and more. At the same time, we have tremendous judgment of people who are wealthy. There is so much guilt tied up with our having things that make life easier and more enjoyable. We want prosperity, but we feel guilty for having it. The exercises in Chapter Four can be very helpful in working through this. You want to reveal, heal, and embrace the shadow self that may be sabotaging your enjoyment of having the prosperity you deserve. Also, there is a very effective program that focuses specifically in this area that I highly recommend. It's Derek Rydall's *Awakened Wealth* program. You can find it on his website: DerekRydall.com/programs.

Health and Well-being

After you have written your Affirmative Prayer and created an Intention Mandala filled with images of vibrant health and well-being—all of which create the conditions in consciousness that welcome wellness—you'll want to spend more time playing in the energy of well-being. To begin that journey, make sure you listen to the Guided Meditation on Health and Well-being found on my website, Breakthrough2.com/meditations. Then, endeavor to create a living environment that fills you with joy. Fill your home with music, color, and fun things that spark joy. Go on a Gratitude Walk daily. Strive to increase time doing what you love by twenty percent. Those activities generate the hormones and neurotransmitters in your body that contribute to a strong immune system.

Also, spend time feeling Life Energy vibrating within every cell of your body. Unity co-founder, Myrtle Fillmore, would imagine all her cells responding to her positive words. She wrote this about her process:

> I began to teach my body and got marvelous results. I told the life in my liver that it was not torpid or inert, but full of vigor and energy. I told the life in my stomach that it was not weak or inefficient but energetic, strong and intelligent. I told the life in my abdomen that it was no longer infested with ignorant thoughts or disease, put there by myself and doctors, but that it was all athrill with the sweet, pure, wholesome energy of God. I told my limbs that they were active and strong. I told my

eyes that they did not see of themselves but that they expressed that sight of Spirit, and that they were drawing on an unlimited source. I told them that they were young eyes, clear, bright eyes, because the light of God shone right through them. I told my heart that the pure love of Christ flowed in and out through its beatings and that all the world felt its joyous pulsations. I went to all the life centers in my body and spoke words of Truth to them—words of strength and power.[1]

It was with this practice that she healed herself of tuberculosis. Of course, she wrote this in nineteenth-century language. But you get the idea. There is wisdom in directing our loving energy and speaking words of truth to all the organs of our body. Making a meditation out of this, or perhaps doing this visualization before you fall asleep, will reap rich rewards.

Most importantly, at the end of the day, conduct a review of your day and see if there is anyone with whom you feel even a twinge of resentment. Lack of forgiveness is a huge contributing factor in chronic conditions. Practice forgiveness daily. Release each and every resentment. It's equally important to practice self-forgiveness. Also, monitor yourself to see if you are trying to ignore or repress strong negative emotions. Remember, those emotions don't go away because you refuse to acknowledge them. They just go underground where they become toxic. So when emotions arise, be sure to do the exercises outlined in Chapter Three to help release them in a healthy way.

In addition, make sure you complete the exercises in this chapter to develop a strong relationship with your inner guidance. Follow that guidance in choosing the healing modality that might be appropriate for you, whether that's medical, alternative treatment, or a combination thereof. Physical healing happens when all levels of your being are engaged in the healing effort—mental/emotional, spiritual, and physical.

And when you feel your condition flair up, or you feel yourself being pulled into doubt, fear or hopelessness, pull out your favorite Pattern Interrupter and go for it.

Career

Let's say you are looking for employment. You want a job that is fulfilling; that utilizes your skills and unique gifts, and that pays well. Or perhaps your desire is to build a successful business doing what you love. Either way, your highest self is calling you to express your gifts in service to others in a way that is joyous and rewarding for all. Work can be one of the most sacred activities we can do. Khalil Gibran put it this way:

> When you work you fulfill a part of earth's furthest dream, assigned to you when that dream was born. And in keeping yourself with labour you are in truth loving life. And to love life through labour is to be intimate with life's inmost secret.[2]

The starting point for the emergence of your highest good in this area is to have an Affirmative Prayer you practice on a regular basis that gets you into the vibrational-field-of-love. From there you claim and accept your heart's desire. Remember, your good is already here as an idea in the mind of the Infinite, and your experience of "desire" is actually the universe knocking at the door of your consciousness saying, "Here it is. This is yours. Please accept it." In addition, you want to view your Intention Mandala daily, which should be filled with images that evoke joyous success.

But let's say that you are currently working in a job that is anything but a dream. Maybe it's boring or stressful and you find yourself watching the clock constantly, just waiting for the moment you can leave. Perhaps you're there just for the paycheck or the benefits. Because you don't love it, you're probably doing the bare minimum to stay employed. Maybe you're thinking, "Well, it's a living." But deep down you know that's not really living. The problem is, your resistance is creating an energy that is, in fact, pushing your desired good further and further away.

Change your idea about your current experience and your experience will change. Rather than thinking of your current work as drudgery, or a necessary evil you need to endure until your "dream job" shows up, think of your time there as an opportunity to give your love and your energy in service to others. Look for ways you can be more helpful to others or your boss. Commit to excellence in all that do, no matter how menial it appears. Answering phones is an opportunity to greet the caller with love and recognize their Divine Self. Entering data, or balancing budgets, is an opportunity to express the quality of Divine order. Washing dishes is an opportunity to bring beauty to your environment. Business meetings are an opportunity to connect with others in Creative Mind and allow solutions to emerge from a realm of infinite possibilities. Every act you perform in your job is an opportunity to be present in the moment, and experience the sacredness of each act.

Making this one change in consciousness will reap enormous rewards because you have jumped into the flow of life energy. You are generating a higher frequency energy that will carry your true heart's desire into manifestation.

Eric Butterworth says in his book, *Spiritual Economics*, "Work is, and should be so considered by every worker, a giving process . . . work in the job is the means by which you build a consciousness of giving, which in turn gives rise to an outworking or 'receiving flow.'"

The Law of Circulation is an exchange of giving and receiving. You cannot hold back in any area and expect abundance to flow. You must initiate the circulation by first giving. Give of your talents, your time, and your treasure. Most importantly, give of your love. As you continue to circulate your gifts into the universe, you open the floodgates for an abundance of good to flow into your life.

Then simply follow your inner guidance and take action following that guidance. Network, take classes to improve your skills, intern, volunteer, follow leads, and most importantly infuse everything you do with love. Embrace the attitude of giving of your time and your love to others. Help others achieve their goals and that energy will circle back to you.

This is how we play in the energy of the answer, even when it's difficult. Applying committed effort into these activities will have the effect of creating a vortex of creative "yes" energy that allows the good you are seeking to flow from the Source within you and into your experience with ease and grace.

We'll now turn our focus to the realization of the highest vision for our lives, and for the world.

10

LIVING ON PURPOSE

You have brains in your head . . . and feet on your shoes.
You can steer yourself in any direction you choose.

—*Theodor Geisel*

The above quote is from one of my favorite poets and philosophers, Theodor Geisel, otherwise known as Dr. Seuss. It confirms the idea of which you are now familiar: We are powerful co-creators in our lives. But it often leads to an unsettling question: In what direction *am* I choosing to go? Is what I'm choosing really the right path for me? Will it be all I'm hoping it will be?

Now, some people have a clear idea about where they're headed and are blissfully walking that path. Others don't have a clue. Some keep switching paths. Still others are just enjoying the ride, wherever it takes them. Ultimately, there's no right or wrong direction to take. Whatever direction you've been walking so far has been the perfect path for you, even if it's been fraught with pain and unhappiness. It's ultimately brought you to this moment.

However, the direction that brings us the greatest joy and sense of fulfillment is the one that expresses our soul's individual imprint— what we're coded for. It's as unique as our individual thumbprint. And the best way to ascertain your individual code is to, as Socrates said, "Know thyself." I'd add to that "love thyself." Knowing and loving yourself is the result of cultivating an ongoing relationship with your Inner Wisdom. It's a process you have already begun. As you continue to develop that relationship, it will continue to reveal the direction that leads you to your true purpose—your reason for being here.

Theologian and mentor to Dr. Martin Luther King Jr., Howard Thurman, once said, "Don't ask what the world needs. Ask what makes you come alive and go do that. What the world needs is more people that have come alive."

Our true purpose is always something that makes us "come alive."

This is the juice of our lives. By doing it, we express our full Divine Potential, which naturally contributes to the whole. Because we are connected together in a beautiful web of life, our true purpose, by its very nature, impacts the world in a positive way. It's no mistake you are here now, at this particular time in history, and awake to a larger reality. There is a quantum shift happening, and the world needs conscious, heart-centered, purpose-driven people committed to helping birth a world that works for everyone. This is living a life of "engaged spirituality." The more each of us lives our true purpose, the more the world heals. Remember our statement of being from Chapter Two, "We are Spiritual Beingness transforming human experience." We transform human experience when we live authentically from an awareness or our spiritual nature.

Sometimes we find our way to our purpose by getting clear about what we *don't* want. In other words, "being pushed by the pain." There's value in reaching the point where we feel that "enough is enough," and we're ready for real change. Pain is often the impetus for transformation. Unfortunately, many get stuck in the problem. They get trapped in a maze of victimhood that makes it difficult to know how to move forward and implement the changes that really work.

What's infinitely more effective is to be *pulled by a vision*. Having a compelling vision serves as a guiding light that leads us out of the maze. Described below is a process for discovering that unique vison for your life. With it you will open to a vision for your own unique version of a fulfilling and rewarding life where you are sharing your particular gifts in service to others. What shape that takes is individual for everyone. Your highest vision could take the expression of a successful career, but it doesn't need to—it could just be a way of life. It could be a commitment to volunteering in a way that expresses your gifts. It could be some creative expression that serves the world in some way.

THE SOUL'S CODE OR THE DREAM OF THE EGO?

For a number of years, I thought I was living my vision. I really believed I was following my unique purpose by owning a business that helped new mothers create a strong, loving bond with their babies, while learning to nurture themselves. I had two women partners in succession. I liked the idea of having my own business that was founded by and run by moms, for moms. It put to use my writing skills as I authored *The Baby Bonding Book*. It encouraged my creative side as I designed fun coupon books to support new mothers, and assembled and sold baby baskets filled with cute organic clothes and products for baby and mom. I even had a radio show interviewing parenting experts.

It was fun for a while, and I am still proud of the book. But the whole experience felt like a colossal struggle. It was fraught with obstacle after obstacle. I had issues with each of the partners not taking the business as seriously as I did. I kept pouring more and more money into the business to try to grow it, but the margins were too slim. Then, just as we were about to sign a fabulous deal with Target for the coupon books, everything started to collapse. In the end the deal fell through, but not before I ordered and paid for 20,000 books.

Coincidently, it was during this time that I was diagnosed with breast cancer. I remember the day the truck came to deliver the pallets of 20,000 books to my house; I had just come home from the hospital after major surgery. I went out to sign for the order in a daze and told the men to stack them all in the garage. Those books filled the entire space from floor to ceiling. There was absolutely no room left for our cars! I spent the next two years knocking on the doors of baby boutiques, trying my best to sell them all. Unfortunately, I earned only enough to pay just the minimum on my credit cards, which quickly led to exponential debt.

Even while having fun writing the books and creating the products, I kept feeling deep down like I was ignoring something important. There was a yearning in my soul that I did my best to ignore. I thought I knew what would make me happy. I was sure I was following the right path and pursuing my dream. It all looked good from the outside: Successful mother-of-twins helping other mothers. Certainly my products did help others, considerably. But I was living someone else's vision. It was a dream of the ego-self and never my true purpose. There was something greater calling me.

I remember my husband saying to me, "You know, you'd make a really good minister. You've spent a lot of time meditating, studying spirituality, and taking classes. You've already completed the Spiritual Practitioner training. Why don't you go all the way? Why don't you go to seminary and become a Unity minister?"

I think I said, "Are you kidding? Do you know how hard ministers work and how little they're paid? No thank you. I'm going to make my fortune in my baby business. You watch." And while I may have believed that at the time, there was a deeper reason I didn't want to pursue the minister path: I was afraid. I was afraid of living such a large life. Who would listen to me? Who am I to tell people how to live an inspired life? That would mean I'd have to fully accept my inner Divinity—and live into that. Yikes!

While I knew it was time to let the business go, I clung to it like a toddler clings to her worn-out blanket. I didn't know how to move forward. I was deeply in debt, and even more deeply stuck in the problem.

After our family moved to North Carolina, we found a Unity center and started attending regularly. I deepened my spiritual practice and doubled up on spiritual classes. Gradually, I began to listen to that inner voice I'd been ignoring for so long. It began to reveal to me a vision of a joyous and fulfilling life as a minister and spiritual leader. After I embraced that vision, the path became clear. My fear began to recede as I accepted my unique inner code. I found an interfaith seminary that aligned with my progressive understanding of religion. All the pieces fell into place and the journey—while intensive—was filled with love and joy. I felt my idea of myself expanding. I embraced my Golden Shadow and began to grow into the person I had only admired in others.

Soon after I completed the seminary, I was offered the position of co-minister at the very spiritual community that helped me accept my vision. After I began my work, a path opened up to complete the training required to be ordained as a Unity minister. It was so clear to me the entire universe was supporting the realization of my vision. Six years after announcing to the world that I would never—could never—do ministry, here I am, a doubly ordained minister. Every experience I ever had, everything I ever learned in my adult life, is serving me in what I'm doing now: From my acting experience, to working survival temp jobs, to bootstrapping a small business, to motivational speaking, to raising children, to negotiating relationships, to marriage, to overcoming cancer, to holding my mother's hand while she died. All the talent, skill, and abilities I possess—many I never even knew I had—are now being put to use in service of others. My life makes sense and I'm the happiest I've ever been. I finally listened to my vision, broke through my resistance, followed inner guidance, and the universe supported me in growing into a person living on purpose.

There is an amazing life waiting to be birthed in, through you and as you right now. Of that I am certain. When you discover it, you will feel as if all the pieces of your life are finally falling into place.

It's time to connect with your highest purpose and learn to live it.

VISIONING PROCESS

The Life Visioning process developed by Rev. Michael Bernard Beckwith, and used extensively in his Agape International Spiritual Center, is a highly effective way to find clarity in your life's purpose. It can also be used to gain clarity on a specific project or endeavor. In fact, Agape was birthed from this visioning process when Rev. Michael put it to use with a small group of committed individuals who gathered in his living room to envision an expansive, diverse, and deeply spiritual community. In his book, *Life Visioning,* Beckwith defines visioning as "an intuitive process for opening and sensitizing consciousness to receive Spirit's vision for one's life."

Visioning is a different process than visualization. Visualization can be a powerful tool for focusing our attention on a specific desired result for the purpose of generating energy around its manifestation. But as I've shared, what we think we want may not be what our soul truly desires. Visioning is more about being in the question and gently allowing an answer to emerge. It opens the door to your unique purpose as well as the unacknowledged gifts that are awaiting your recognition. Visioning works as you open your mind, and your heart, to view yourself from the highest possible perspective. You then catch the vision of yourself as a magnificent, glorious being, here on this earth, at this particular time, for a specific purpose.

Once you've identified what your vision is, you'll want to nurture it. You want to encourage it to emerge. This is different from wishing, hoping, or dreaming. You are *consciously inviting* your vision to naturally blossom. As you move forward, notice how your actions are either moving you toward, or away, from your vision. Commit to moving in the direction your vision points.

LESSON TEN, EXERCISE ONE: VISIONING

The visioning process I offer here is similar to the Live Visioning process developed by Beckwith, with my own added twist. You can find the guided process by going to Breakthrough2.com/Exercises: Lesson 10, Exercise 1

1. Get comfortable. Make sure you won't be disturbed for the next 20 minutes or so. Get quiet, and start breathing slowly and deeply.
2. Center your awareness in your heart. Consciously open to that Divine Love at your heart-center. Feel that love growing and radiating through your body and eventually surrounding you in a blanket of love. Allow yourself to bask in that love for a few minutes.
3. Now, invite your Inner Wisdom to reveal the overall vision for your life. Ask, "What is my unique purpose?" Then just listen.
4. You might want to further ask: "What gifts and innate abilities do I have that are activated when I am living my purpose? How does this vision 'make me come alive?' When I am living my purpose, how does that serve humanity?" Then, open to the feeling of it. What does it look like? What does it feel like? What does it sound like? How might my living this vision impact others? Go slow and allow the answers to bubble up.
5. Then ask: "What do I need to let go of in order to live this vision?" And listen.
6. Finally, ask: "What is my growing edge? Or, what qualities must I embody to be in alignment with this highest vision?" Again, just listen.

When you feel that you've received something, open your eyes, grab your journal, and take a few moments to write down whatever you received—words, images, full sentences—whatever. Or use the space below to write what you've received.

_____

_____

_____

_____

_____

_____

_____

Now, make a list of all the talents, skills, and abilities you have, as well as what you've learned from previous experiences, which will serve you as you live this vision.

1. _____

2. _____

3. _____

4. _____

5. _____

6. _____

7. _____

8. _____

9. _____

10. _____

Pay close attention to steps five and six. These are important steps that make this process uniquely effective. Growth always involves leaving behind what you have been accustomed to and what may have been comfortable. This can be anything from old beliefs or an attitude that no longer fits, to behaviors or ways of being that may have supported you in the past, but will not serve you as you grow into living your vision. It may even be a relationship that has been holding you back from your ability to be fully you, or a previous plan you were using to guide you. Don't assume you know what it is. Listen to the guidance of your Inner Wisdom.

In step six you are asking your Inner Wisdom to reveal areas of growth that need to be embraced in order to be the person who is living on purpose. This can be a very exciting part of the process. Remember, the universe will support whatever growth is required of you. Also, know that as you begin to express your full Divine Potential, it is natural to have resistance. Growth and change are scary. Expanding our sense of self involves stepping way out of our comfort zone. But we don't need to let that deter us when we employ the following tools.

DEALING WITH FEAR

Most people spend their lives living in a little box of what they think is possible for them and what they think they can handle. The box is comfortable and familiar, so most stay there. They don't need to face their fears, or think of trying new things. It's safe. But it's stifling, and it's liable to get really small and feel terribly cramped. Ultimately, it's not really living. We are part of the ever-expanding nature of the universe and we ourselves are meant to grow and expand. We are meant to grow into our full Divine Potential and express our true magnificent self.

If you have gotten this far in this book, my guess is you are somewhere in the process of breaking out of your constricting box. Even if you have spent your life living too small, you are now ready to break free and grow into your highest possible self. Either way, you know that growing and expanding your sense of self can be challenging and scary. The ego wants us to stay small, and its voice is loud. Maybe you've been tempted to shrink back. There are moments we all want to jump back into our comfortable little boxes. And yet, there is that Divine yearning within you that keeps you moving forward. Trust that impulse. It will support you the entire way.

When you begin to move forward in the direction of your high-est vision, and feel that fear at the pit of your stomach, know that this feeling is an affirmation that you are growing. It's a signal that you are moving in the right direction. You are stretching. You are spreading your wings and getting ready to take off. Continue to breathe through it and say, "Yes!" knowing that the universe has your back. If you should be tempted to shrink back and feel that you are not up to the task, remind yourself that you are no longer relying on the little ego-self to meet the challenge. There is a larger, Limitless Self within you that is leading the way. Affirm: "I, of my little self, steps back and I allow my larger, Divine Self to lead the way now."

It is also very helpful to find support during this growth phase. Consider who among your friends can be a true ally in your expan-sion. How can they support you in realizing your vision? See if you can set up a regular time to connect and support each other. Maybe you have a group of friends who can offer support, encouragement, and share tips. During one of the largest growth spurts in my life, I met regularly with a group of women who were also on a similar journey. We gathered at a favorite restaurant, taking up a whole back corner, and spent three hours at a time eating while sharing information, tips, tears, fears, and our love and support. I grew significantly because of it. A decade after we all moved in different directions, I still count each one as an ally and friend. If you don't have a group like this, create one. It will change your life. Just make sure they are heart-centered and truly have your best interests at heart—and you theirs.

Expanding your sense of self involves releasing old ideas, beliefs, behaviors, and ways of being that are no longer serving you, while growing into new ones. This growth is challenging and will likely raise your resistance. You might find it helpful to engage the assistance of a life coach or a spiritual coach—someone who can spot patterns you may not even see and help you to transcend them. They can be a dedicated ally, encouraging you as you move through your fear. If your vision involves stepping into a leadership role, go for it! Your coach can help you hone the skills that make an effective leader.

Above all, keep practicing. Put into daily practice the principles of this book. Go back to the list of Pattern Interrupters and put them to use. Review the exercises and processes from previous chapters, selecting the ones that support you best, *and keep working*. Regular, consistent practice is the nourishment that supports the emergence of your full Divine Potential. Here's what New Thought mystic Joel Goldsmith wrote in his book, *Practicing the Presence*, about the importance of practice:

> It is possible for anyone to change the trend of his life, not by hearing or reading truth, but by making it an active part of his consciousness in daily experience, until it becomes a habit every moment of the day, instead of an occasional thought. Let these principles operate in consciousness morning, noon and night, until gradually the actual awareness comes. Then we make the transition from being hearers of the Word to being doers of the Word. Then we shall be abiding in the Word and shall bear fruit richly.[1]

And so, we come full circle. Our original premise is that there is nothing to fix. You are perfect exactly as you are. It's more about discovering and embracing the fullness of who you are, gently releasing what has been covering up the masterpiece and aligning all levels of your being with your true Spiritual Self. The more you do, the more life opens up, and the magnificence within you can more fully blossom. And you become a person who lives on purpose.

Know that I am here for you and holding you in my Affirmative Prayers. Connect with me on social media or send me an email and let me know how you are progressing. If you would like spiritual coaching to support you on your journey, I would be happy to assist you. You'll find a variety of ways to work with me on my site, under the Coaching tab, and the Classes tab.

ENDNOTES

A HUNK OF ROCK OR A MASTERPIECE EMERGING?

1. Gay Hendricks, *Learning to Love Yourself,* (New York: Atria Books, 1982), 30.

EVOLVING OUR FOUNDATION

1. Ralph Waldo Emerson, *The Over-Soul,* (New York: American Classics Library), 5.
2. Warren Felt Evans, *The Primitive Mind Cure,* (New York: H.H. Carter & Co Publisher, 1885), 40.
3. Emma Curtis Hopkins, *Scientific Christian Mental Practice* (Camarillo, CA DeVorss & Company Publishers, 1958), 66.
4. H. Emilie Cady, *Lessons in Truth,* (Unity Village, MO: Unity Books, 1903), 98.
5. Cady, 77.
6. Myrtle Fillmore, *How to Let God Help You,* (Unity Village, MO: Unity Books, 1956), 60.
7. Charles Fillmore, *Christian Healing,* (Unity Village, MO: Unity Books, 1909), 14.

8. Ernest Holmes, *The Science of Mind*, (United Kingdom: Martino Fine Books, 2011, Reprint of 1926 edition), 391.
9. Thomas Shepherd, *Friends in High Places*, (Bloomington, IN: iUniverse, 2004), 79.
10. Emma Curtis Hopkins, *Scientific Christian Mental Practice*, (Camarillo, CA, DeVorss & Company Publishers, 1958), 69.
11. Charles Fillmore, a talk entitled: *The Undisciplined States of Consciousness*, (April 12, 1931).
12. Michael Bernard Beckwith, *Spiritual Liberation*, (New York: Atria Books, 2008), 36.
13. Paul Hasselbeck, *Point of Power*, (San Antonio, TX: Prosperity Publishing House, 2007), 26.
14. Gregg Braden, *The Divine Matrix*, (Carlsbad, CA: Hay House, 2007), 3.

WE ARE MULTIDIMENSIONAL BEINGS

1. Myrtle Fillmore, *How to Let God Help You* (Unity Village, MO: Unity Books, 1956).

THE SHADOWY FRIEND

1. Charles Fillmore, *The Revealing Word*, (Unity Books, First Edition 1959), 32.
2. Debbie Ford, *The Dark Side of the Light Chasers*, (New York: Riverhead Books, 1998), 40.
3. Derek Rydall, *Emergence, Seven Steps for Radical Life Change*, (New York: Atria Books, 2015), 143.

FORGIVENESS GIVES TO US

1. Dr. Jim Dincalci, *How to Forgive When You Can't: The Breakthrough Guide to Free Your Heart & Mind,* (The Forgiveness Foundation, Chapel Hill, NC 2010), 14.

ENDNOTES

2. Mary Manin Morrissey, *Building Your Field of Dreams,* (Bantam Books, New York, 1996), 160.

3. *A Course in Miracles,* (Foundation for Inner Peace, 1975), Textbook Chapter 14–IV and Workbook Lesson 122.

4. Charles Fillmore, *Jesus Christ Heals,* (Unity Village, MO: Unity Books, First Edition 1939), 60.

UNDER THE INFLUENCE (OF THE COLLECTIVE UNCONSCIOUS)

1. Carl Jung, *Analytical Psychology: Its Theory and Practice: The Tavistock Lectures,* (1935).

2. Dave DeLuca, *Pathways to Joy: The Master Vivekananda on The Four Yoga Paths to God* (Novato, IL: New World Library, 2003), 10.

3. Painter, Kim. *As Births Decline in Young Women They Keep Rising in 40-somethings, Here's Why. USA Today,* May 19, 2018. April 2020.

THE TRANSFORMATIONAL DIMENSION

1. Ralph Waldo Emerson, *Journals and Miscellaneous Notebooks,* 5:18.

2. Abhishiktananda, *Saccidananda: A Christian Approach to Advaitic Experience,* (Delhi: ISPCK, 1974), 78.

3. Myrtle Fillmore, *Myrtle Fillmore's Healing Letters,* (Compiled by Frances W. Foulks, Unity Village, MO: Unity Books), 1948, 32.

PLAYING IN THE ENERGY OF THE ANSWER

1. Wallace D. Wattles, *The Science of Getting Rich* (Atria Book, New York, 2007, Originally published 1910 by Elizabeth Towne Publishing, New York), 47.

187

PLAYING IN THE ANSWER WHEN IT'S CHALLENGING

1. Myrtle Fillmore, *How to Let God Help You*, (Unity Village, MO: Unity Books, 1956), Chapter 23.
2. Khalil Gabran, *The Prophet*, (New York: Knopf, 1923), 25-26.

LIVING ON PURPOSE

1. Joel S. Goldsmith, *Practicing the Presence*, (New York: Harper-Collins, 1958), 26.

ACKNOWLEDGMENTS

Without the love, support, and encouragement of my spiritual family at Unity Center Peace, I would have never completed this book. They keep me focused on what's truly important. An abundance of gratitude goes to each one of them.

A special thank you goes to my mentor and teacher for the last 25 years, Rev. Michael Bernard Beckwith. He opened my mind and put a fire in my heart that launched a desire in me to reach my highest vision.

There are guiding lights and agents of healing in everyone's experience that can change the course of a life in a positive direction. In my life those people include Rev. Marlene Morris, Angela C. Montano, Rev. Martha Dewing, Derek Rydall, and Rev. Linda Martella-Whitsett. Much gratitude to each of these beautiful souls.

Much gratitude goes to my husband, Dana, who offers continuous love and support. And to my fabulous daughters, Olivia and Juliet who help ground me in the "real world."

I owe a debt of gratitude to the musician who provided, gratis, his beautiful arrangements to all the guided meditations that accompany this book, Phillip Pennington.

Lastly, I am grateful for all of you who are willing to do the work. I acknowledge your willingness to face the places that have kept you stuck, and the courage to allow your magnificence to emerge. Your willingness makes it easier for others to shine their own light, and ultimately, for the world to awaken.

ABOUT THE AUTHOR

Victoria Loveland-Coen has been a student of New Thought/ Ancient Wisdom for over 35 years. She was initiated into Transcendental Meditation at the age of 16 and has continued the practice throughout her life. She is doubly ordained, first from One Spirit in New York as an interfaith/interspiritual minister, and secondly, from Unity Worldwide Ministries as a Unity Minister. She is currently serving as the Senior Minister at Unity Center of Peace in Chapel Hill.

Victoria founded The Gratitude Experiment where she supports followers in their practice of Proactive Gratitude. She has written two books: *Manifesting Your Desires* and *The Baby Bonding Book*. As an inspirational speaker, teacher, and spiritual coach, her passion is to help others experience their spiritual magnificence, while permanently eliminating self-sabotaging blocks, so they can live their true life's purpose.

Victoria lives in Chapel Hill with her writer/producer/professor husband, Dana Coen, and has twin daughters in college.

Victoria would love to stay in touch with you. You can connect with her by going to:

www.Breakthrough2.com

email: Victoria@ManifestYourGood.com

Facebook: The Gratitude Experiment

Instagram: lovelandcoen

Twitter: @ManifestingMama